Jethro Tull

MINSTREL IN THE GALLERY

In-depth

Laura Shenton

Jethro Tull

MINSTREL IN THE GALLERY

In-depth

Laura Shenton

WP
WYMER
PUBLISHING
Bedford, England

First published in 2021 by Wymer Publishing
Bedford, England www.wymerpublishing.co.uk Tel: 01234 326691
Wymer Publishing is a trading name of Wymer (UK) Ltd

Print edition (fully illustrated): **ISBN: 978-1-912782-81-9**

Edited by Jerry Bloom.

eBook formatting by Coinlea.

A catalogue record for this book is available from the British Library.

Typeset by Andy Bishop / 1016 Sarpsborg
Cover design by 1016 Sarpsborg.

Contents

Preface   7

Chapter One: *Why Minstrel In The Gallery?*   9

Chapter Two: *The Making Of Minstrel In The Gallery*   31

Chapter Three: *Playing Live In 1975*   53

Chapter Four: *The Legacy Lives On*   67

Appendices   103
    Personnel
    Time Signatures
    Track Listing
    Discography
    Tour Dates

Preface

There's a fair bit that has already been written on Jethro Tull, both biographically and from a music analysis perspective. On such basis, you could be thinking, "Another Tull book? Really?" But here's the thing; I do think there is a gap in the literature whereby the biographical stuff out there doesn't talk in length about the music and the music analysis stuff out there often makes a lot of connections between Jethro Tull's music and theories that haven't actually been put out there (or indeed corroborated) by the band themselves.

So I'm not trying to reinvent the wheel here; what I want to do is offer an insight into *Minstrel In The Gallery* in a way that discusses the music in detail in relation to what the band's intentions were. I want to offer something factual rather than something that is peppered with my own opinion and interpretation of the music. You won't see any of that whole kind of "this section is in the key of C and it therefore means X" or "I think this lyric means Y". For of course, the beauty of a lot of Jethro Tull's music is the ambiguity. As author of this book, it is not my place to throw a lot of my own opinions out there because it won't add anything to the literature if I do that.

The purpose of this book is to look at *Minstrel In The Gallery* in detail; an extent of detail that has been put out there by Ian Anderson in terms of what was intended by the album and detail as in how the album was perceived at the time. As a result, throughout this book you're going to see lots of quotes from vintage articles. I think it's important to corroborate such material as there will probably come a time when it is harder to source.

To address something that often comes up in Jethro Tull fan conversation, there is often debate surrounding whether the band consisted of Ian Anderson plus other musicians or whether it was a group of musicians who contributed equally. This book contains a lot of quotes from Ian Anderson; proportionately a lot more than from any other member of Jethro Tull. This isn't due to the fact that I am saying, "Ian Anderson is Jethro Tull and the other musicians' input isn't important", not at all! It's simply the case that of all the members of Jethro Tull, Ian Anderson has done the vast majority of interviews as the mainstay and founding member of the band and both vintage and recent interviews are reflective of that.

A quick note on names and spellings; John Evans sometimes went by the name of John Evan. He was quoted in *Jackie* in August 1970 when asked if John Evan was his real name; "Almost — this is the name that just sort of came out. I'd done some session work for the last Jethro Tull LP, and when the sleeve came out there'd been a spelling mistake — and they called me John Evan. My real name is John Evans. But everybody calls me Evan now."

Similarly, Jeffery Hammond adopted the name "Hammond-Hammond" as a joke, as both his father's name and mother's maiden name were the same. Of course, David Palmer is now Dee Palmer. In all cases, I've transcribed their names as they were written in each original instance.

In the interest of transparency, I have no affiliation with Jethro Tull or with any of their associates. This book is based on extensive research and objective commentary.

Chapter One

Why Minstrel In The Gallery?

The early seventies was musically and commercially a prosperous time for Jethro Tull. In 1971 the success of *Aqualung* propelled the band to global success and this was exemplified with their 1972 album, *Thick As A Brick*.

After *Thick As A Brick*, *A Passion Play* was representative of a bad patch for the band. It was largely panned at the time. Combined with the fact that Jethro Tull were fed up of touring at that point, there were plenty of rumours afloat that the band were going to call it quits entirely.

In 1974, the *War Child* album signified that Jethro Tull were back into the swing of things but it wasn't until 1975 with *Minstrel In The Gallery* that the band was just starting to get back on their feet again. The story of *Minstrel In The Gallery* surrounds a band who, having taken a lull in terms of popularity, made an album that was largely inspired by aggression and frustration. The end result is a strong piece of work that features Jethro Tull really starting to rock out again.

The album has an edge to it that embraces intense use of guitar from Martin Barre and equally assertive organ playing from John Evans. And yet, there are plenty of gentle acoustic moments too, all tied in with clever and witty lyrics from Ian Anderson. *Minstrel In The Gallery* warrants further discussion because it was born out of a turbulent time in Jethro Tull's tenure and yet musically, it offers so much.

Anderson was quoted in *Down Beat* in March 1976; "Well, you see, *War Child* was done after first having taken a long time off the road. For six months, we didn't play concerts and *War Child* was like getting back together with the guys in the group after three months of not even seeing each other very much, then saying, 'Right, we have to start rehearsing a new album' — It was like entering a new phase of the group's existence. I enjoyed playing fairly simple, shortish pieces of music — a sort of renewing thing, another cycle. It was an enjoyable album to make, a very easy album to make. It had a good vibe to it."

"Then we had a single from it ('Bungle In The Jungle') which was a very catchy, sort of commercial sound as far as all the disc jockeys were concerned. So everyone sort of thought, well Jethro Tull is back playing it safe, doing something nice and inoffensive. For us, it was absolutely the right thing to do at the time, because that was the mood. Since then, there has been lots of personal, emotional, and domestic problems with members of the group. It's a different mood now."

"*Minstrel In The Gallery* is much more intense, much more introverted, much more a solitude. It may again be seen as a totally sort of uncommercial thing. People may really not like it. And I shall be somewhat despondent and disappointed if people don't enjoy it. But finally, I have to do what I want to do. Otherwise, we have no possible excuse for getting together, me and the audience. We have no reason under the sun to even breathe the same air, unless it's the result of me saying I'm playing what I want to play because I actually have to cope with this and say it for whatever obscure or selfish set of personal reasons. So there exists a coincidence where other people derive some enjoyment or some emotional sort of reward from that. That's all it amounts to really, a coincidence, because I'm not terribly responsible when it comes to catering to what people want."

Minstrel In The Gallery is the result of post lull Jethro Tull, at least in terms of the band's relationship with the media at the time. Regarding the lyric, "I have no time for *Time Magazine* or

Rolling Stone" in 'Baker Street Muse', Anderson said in 2019; "Having been on the cover of both, these were hugely important back then, as was being fortunate enough to get the attention of John Peel. But of course they'd fall out of love with you as quickly as they'd fallen in. *Rolling Stone* swiftly decided we were the spawn of the devil because we weren't Americana. And eventually John Peel decreed we were off his Christmas card list and never spoke to me again. I was mortified, really. It was painful to feel suddenly cut off... I'd learned long before to recognise that you can have everybody reckoning you're the Next Great Thing. Then within a year or two get some poisonously negative stuff. And this was in the days before social media! Imagine the vitriol and condemnation and abuse now if I'd come out with *A Passion Play*. But yes, it was up and down, up and down, all the time."

Having achieved tremendous commercial success with *Aqualung* and *Thick As A Brick*, Jethro Tull were welcomed by fans and the media alike. They were generally considered to be popular, fresh and exciting and were embraced by the people who presumably mattered to them. However, the extent to which *Passion Play* was panned was chronically harsh and whilst *War Child* did a little better, it still carries the legacy of a failed movie project that never came to be.

In an interview with BBC Radio in 1979, Anderson explained; "In fact, the *War Child* album came out of the music that was written ostensibly for a film, a feature film, the fairly lengthy synopsis of which I wrote, which followed about three, four, five months of various negotiations behind getting that film to its pre-production stage, i.e. finding a director, finding — or at least soliciting — the promised assistance of the two key actors that I had in mind, and one or two other people who were going to become involved with script writing, dancing, choreography and so on."

"It was a very allegorical kind of plot, and one which I don't think had very much commercial viability, at least inasmuch as the big American companies were concerned. When we went to them with the idea of the script they were quite keen to go ahead, but they of course wanted the right of the final cut and they wanted a degree of control over both the casting and the director, which I wasn't prepared to give away."

"Basically when it came to getting the money out of the Yanks — and of course there wasn't the money at that point in time in the British film industry, and I certainly wasn't going to put any of mine in, on such a ludicrous project as making a film — basically they wanted 'stars', you know, it's the same old story. Very quickly I became disenchanted with the whole thing and decided that if it really couldn't be done with that rather gracious sense of people doing something they all felt mutually involved with then I really didn't want to do it at all. So we called a halt to the proceedings, and out of the music that had been begun we rearranged it as the group album *War Child*."

Anderson continued, "The *War Child* theme — the theme of the movie — was very closely related to *Passion Play*, which I think I said earlier on was the idea of what might happen to you when you die, exploring the different avenues of heaven and hell, of rightness, wrongness, and options of where one goes in the afterlife: a mixture of all sorts of half-baked religious ideas of the past and my own half-baked ideas thrown in for good measure."

"The *War Child* thing was really the story of that: a story about a young girl who was killed in a car crash at the beginning of the movie, and immediately after that first two or three minutes' worth of present-day reality then jumps into the wide unknown of an allegory, which is difficult for people to swallow anyway, which dealt with the idea of there being a heaven and hell, but in terms of the movie they were set in the context of very real places. It was set in a middling-sized town where the town council, the people who ran the town, were divided into two factions which had some vague similarity between left wing and right wing movements, but there wasn't a question of being 'goodies' and 'baddies' because what I was really trying to say in the film was that it's not a question of God being good and the Devil being bad because the roles are very often interchangeable."

"I mean, God comes in turning people to pillars of salt, and the Devil quite often gives people a good time with the odd pagan festival or whatever. I'm not saying the roles are really interchangeable, but I just attempted to explore the idea that the Devil might not necessarily be such a bad guy: he was full of the same human frailties as the rest of us. And God for that matter, who got himself very mixed up in the movie, trying to keep things on the straight and beaten track."

"The songs (on *War Child*) aren't linked, and it's not a concept album in as much as it's not putting across any real story; there's not very much similarity in the style of the music on the album. It's a concept album only in as much as it does have behind it this unifying theme, but rather than put that across without the movie to back it up it seemed better just to leave that out of the equation altogether and present the music as a collection of songs. On the one hand there was a feeling that *War Child* was another concept album which was even more devious than the last two, and on the other hand there was a feeling that it was a cop-out back to the original 'lots of nice little songs' approach, and it even had a hit single on it."

"At least it was a hit in America: 'Bungle In The Jungle'. I suppose it seemed a much more commercial recording than the two or three albums previous to it… 'Bungle In The Jungle' has, so they tell me, an infectious rhythm — I know several people were treated for it. It was one of the few real hits that we had in America, probably because it had that disco appeal. It concerned me a bit at the time actually, because I never thought of Jethro Tull as a group that anyone could dance to except me!

And suddenly we had a song out which was being played on all the radio stations which presumably people were boogying to in discotheques, and I was horrified having to witness the end result of all that."

"The song is actually just about the cruelty of life, the animal life in the city — it sounds a bit trite to talk about it — maybe it was even more trite to sing about it, I don't know. I'm sure I have my critics who would say yes, that was the case. But then I always seem to write those sort of songs which invite criticism; Jethro Tull is the sort of group which invites criticism just by being what it is. I hope it's because people expect a lot from Jethro Tull that we do get our fair share of criticism, and inevitably having a lot expected from you, you tend to disappoint a certain number of people a certain part of the time. For everyone who likes Jethro Tull there's always somebody else who absolutely hates it. I suppose that's quite a healthy situation, and I probably do a bit to encourage that by, oh, inventing titles like *Too Old To Rock 'n' Roll: Too Young To Die*."

In the same interview, Anderson said of 'Skating Away On The Thin Ice Of The New Day'; "It's a song which I think is basically a song of optimism: setting off as things are crumbling around you, rather bravely setting off across (in terms of the lyrics) the thin ice of the new day. Making a total clean sweep. I always saw Martin Barre, at least on the album cover, as being the one who ought to appear to be skating away, because he's fairly optimistic about things and bravely ventures into them like... paying over the odds for a second-hand Bentley or whatever and finding out it doesn't work properly, there's no engine inside it or something."

Although the film from which *War Child* evolved was abandoned, a certain amount of the film score was recorded. In the interview with BBC Radio in 1979, Anderson said; "We recorded quite a bit of the music, because someone like me can't just jump into the movie industry and announce that I'm going to be largely responsible for getting a full-length feature film together and spending at least a million dollars of somebody else's money without putting the cards on the table and saying 'Here's what I have to give'. So we made a demo version of some of the orchestral music, which included a pastoral but nonetheless moving version of the *War Child* theme itself, which is typical movie-credit music. In fact the only way people have heard that, and we've never really announced that they have been listening to it, but we have, for a couple of years, played the *War Child* orchestral theme while the audience is coming in, taking their seats in auditoriums and so on. Other snippets of the music are what we've used as the intro to our coming on stage during the concert, just two or three minutes of loud music before we come on. So in fact quite a lot of that music has been heard over the last three years, but we've never told anyone who it was. Until now!"

Anderson told *Guitar World* in September 1999; "'Bungle In The Jungle', which is perhaps the best-known song off *War Child*, was the key track for the aborted project we began in France. It's a rather odd song for Jethro Tull, I think. Every so often there are those songs that fall into the conventional pop-rock structure — songs like 'Teacher', for instance — but that style isn't our forte. We're not very good at it because I'm not that kind of a singer, and it doesn't come easy to me to do that stuff. But 'Bungle' was one of those songs that was nice to have done. It's got the Jethro Tull ingredients, but it's a little more straight-ahead. It's Jethro Tull in tight leather trousers."

Whilst *War Child* did come with the hit single, 'Bungle In The Jungle' as well as the classic Jethro Tull song, 'Skating Away On The Thin Ice Of The New Day', it was generally the case that by 1974, many considered the band to be old hat. So much so that in the interview with BBC Radio in 1979, Anderson said; "After the misguided attempt to gain some public sympathy behind that record company-instigated retirement story, it did in fact appear — if you looked at our British or American schedule — that we had in fact disappeared from the scene. However, what we were in fact doing was being engaged on a tour of the Far East and beginning the writing and recording of the *War Child* album."

It is very plausible that the retirement rumours were blown up to sound bigger than the reality of what was really going on. Anderson said to Australian *Go Set* in August 1974; "Well the retirement only lasted for the first weekend really. We split up on a Friday on the plane a reformed again on Monday after breakfast. When I phoned the others and said that we were going into the studio and that we should all go together. It was not really a retirement, we were back together as a group after a couple of weeks of rehearsing, and working on a whole lot of things, I mean different types of music. We spent a long time in the studio, doing about two and a half albums worth of music of various sorts from which we picked the obvious connected material. It was connected in the sense of what 'they' refer to as a concept album. We stuck it all together and it will come out as the next group album called *War Child*."

When asked to explain the rumours about him retiring after the *Passion Play* era of his career, Anderson told *New Musical Express* in February 1975; "I'd been working very hard and was feeling a bit sorry for myself. After touring America alone nineteen times, not counting Europe, Britain and everywhere else, I thought we had to switch off the motor. It was time to take stock of the situation, and I think that's something most groups probably do more frequently than they let on. In our case, since we're so busy, it was necessary to formalise taking that rest. If you actually say 'I really want to stop' to your manager and your agents and all those people, they realise you're not joking. Plus we were talking about doing a movie, so it seemed like a good idea to use that as an explanation. At least we weren't going to vegetate or live in vast country estates with servants and carriages or whatever it is people imagine British rock stars do."

"In the end, the period when we were stopped was something ridiculous like two days. It seems like a big thing to say, but for two days the group did not exist. It was the first time in five years that I could say 'I am not part of the thing called Jethro Tull' for two days — that was an amazing, free feeling. Then I knew it was time to work again. Though we had no definite plans about touring, we started to write a lot of different kinds of music and lay the groundwork for the *War Child* movie. Of the music we were making, some would inevitably come out in the new album, some would be thrown away, and some was just not the sort of thing we could release under the Jethro Tull name. People would run out and buy it without listening to it, take it home and probably be very disappointed because it was radically different from what they expected. I don't mind disappointing people from time to time. I don't like to trade too much on previous success. But also I don't want to take advantage of people and pour something down their throats that they couldn't possibly enjoy. We've made a lot of music that people could not possibly have enjoyed."

Anderson was quoted in *Circus* in December 1975; "If somebody says, 'I think your music is shitty', that's like saying, 'I think your wife's a whore' — And I get very angry when people say that behind my back or via the unassailable media of the press. Because I'm not in a position to defend it and I won't be brought out or taunted by public criticism into answering it back in the same medium. Because I can never win, I'm not a journalist, and I'm not in a position to see that my words remain undistorted or in the true context when they finally appear in print. I don't have the same control of that sort of expression in its final form as I do on record or performing onstage. So I'm naturally wary of being drawn out. And I have a fairly low opinion of the press because I think it plays way below the average level of intelligence of the audience who reads it. I think it sets out purely to survive with the basest instincts of survival. And that about answers everything I have to say anticipating your questions about my attitude towards the press and why I don't do many interviews."

In *New Musical Express* in February 1975, Anderson ironically spoke of his reluctance to give interviews; "If I was into loud and fervent discussions of politics or whatever, maybe I would have had something to talk about. Musically, I felt I had said it all. I don't like to talk about very much other than the music because that's — believe it or not — pretty well all I do. I spent at least an hour last night trying to convince somebody at a radio station here in LA that I don't have any hobbies. I have no spare time. I usually don't know what day it is. In the rare case that I do have a spare evening, I spend it watching the news. That's my idea of a night off. But this radio guy was sure I was lying. My recreation comes entirely within a musical framework. Going into a studio and touring is a recreational thing for me. Especially touring. It's fun! Air-conditioned motorcars, nice airplanes, a Bloody Mary every morning after I wake up, scrambled eggs and bacon, coffee and toast... I don't have any of that at home. My life has become an easy going, fun existence. I love recording, rehearsing, writing, playing and setting up a tour. That's really what I do all year. That's what I've been doing the last year and-a-half since our previous American tour. I haven't stopped playing music except for one weekend when we split up."

"I just don't want to start people off on trying to figure out what this newest album (*War Child*) means in relation to *Passion Play* and the movie idea. They all relate. I just don't want to have to start explaining. I do know, believe it or not, but there's no need for a big intellectual analysis. I'd rather the people just listened to the last two Tull albums as pieces of music... I'd be less than human if my blood didn't boil when some punk kid writer — hardly out of his nappies — has the gall to say our music is bad or unimaginative. I find the use of unqualified, brutal adjectives such as those totally irresponsible."

"Journalists are a terribly destructive lot... Last year, the pop papers descended upon not only Jethro Tull but on a few other groups — and most of it had to do with their unwillingness to give interviews every six months. In a small country like Britain, it's hard to get out of meeting that quota without causing bad feelings. But really, after six months, there's not much to say that you didn't say six months before... I mean, I quite accept that an important album has to be reviewed whether the critic likes it or not, but they should at least offer some criticism. I've had a lot of adverse criticism which has ultimately been good for me."

"Actually, I've always thought of Jethro as a live band anyway. We sell records as souvenirs. When people offer criticism as a sort of entertainment designed to shock or be brutal or cynical or aggressive, that's repulsive. I know that the last few records have been difficult to listen to the first ten times around. This new one (*War Child*), so I'm told, is a lot more accessible. That's just the luck of the draw, because in actual fact, the music isn't any more simple than it's been in the past. Some of it is, but most of it isn't. The lyrics are more obscure than anything I've ever written. But apparently they sound straightforward to other people. That's very, very interesting, but also distinctly worrying to me. I don't know if I like the idea of having made an album people think is easy listening. They'll think 'Oooooh, this is a great rock record' and that'll be the only conclusion they'll draw from it. But it isn't as simple as it appears. I'm a little worried that people will accidentally think *War Child* is a return to a style we've already covered. I can't help it if some of the songs are catchy."

In more recent interviews, Anderson has been less enthusiastic about *Passion Play* but importantly, he said in *Circus* in December 1975; "I mean the best album as a whole I think is definitely *Passion Play*. But there are other albums which have some pretty stuff which doesn't hold up any longer, they have some little things which are accidentally very fine things. *Aqualung* had some good bits on and *War Child* and *Minstrel In The Gallery* have some good bits on, but I think overall they don't stand up as a whole thing the way *Passion Play* did. It was a total emotional thing for me from the beginning to the end — it's very gripping and I'm very honestly moved by it. I hear it about once a year; I've heard it a couple times since it came out, and I've actually been incredibly moved by it both times. Having forgotten the arrangement and what the music was doing, I found it a very energised sort of music. I'm well pleased with that aspect of it."

As much as *Aqualung* had raised the band's public profile in 1971, by 1975, it seems that Anderson was thinking way beyond that one album. He certainly dismissed the notion that *Aqualung* was the definitive album behind Jethro Tull's success. "I think that's a rather simplistic way of looking at it, if you'll forgive me saying so," he explained to *New Musical Express* in February 1975. "I really believe that most of the success of the group has come from the fact that we've played a hell of a lot. That particular album I don't dislike, but it's certainly not our best. *Aqualung* just puts a signpost on a certain point in time. Tull had arrived. A lot of people began to know the name. People started thinking I was Jethro Tull: 'Hey Tull. Hey man. Hey Jethro. Hey Jet.' I once got called 'Jet', which I thought was quite attractive, I must admit. It wasn't by a girl unfortunately — it was by a rather diseased-looking young gentleman from one of the Southern states."

"I, however, disowned the name because it would have been unfair to the others to presume for a moment that people calling me 'Jethro Tull' was anything other than a misguided attempt to indicate friendliness. It's a name which rightfully belongs to all five of us. I'm the only survivor from the original group, but we all get paid the same money. We all have the same stake in it, we all have the same share of the expenses. So I don't really like it too much if people think I'm Jethro Tull. It's funny, but I worry that the rest of the guys will get to feel that they're a group behind me. That's not the case. The case is that I'm the unfortunate singer stuck in front of them."

Recorded in April and released in September 1975, *Minstrel In The Gallery* was Jethro Tull's eighth studio album. It went in a different direction to *War Child*; instead of a wide use of orchestration (such as saxophone, accordion and synthesisers), the album made effective use of a string section conducted by David Palmer (technically it was a string quintet because there is a total of four violins and one cello featured on the album but there are instances in which it is just a quartet playing).

Jethro Tull also went back to using a balanced mix of electric and acoustic pieces; more like in the early seventies with *Benefit*, *Aqualung* and *Thick As A Brick*. Nevertheless, *Minstrel In The Gallery* took the band forwards; it includes some of the their most popular and long serving tracks — 'Minstrel In The Gallery', 'Cold Wind To Valhalla', 'Black Satin Dancer' and 'Baker Street Muse'.

As was reported in *Down Beat* in March 1976; "On *War Child*, Anderson returned to the conventional song lengths; another single, the bouncy 'Bungle In The Jungle', soared to the top of the charts last year. *Minstrel In The Gallery* appeared next, seemingly something of a compromise between the commercial and the more experimental sides to Anderson's ambitions. Along with shorter, catchy songs like 'Cold Wind To Valhalla', the album includes 'Baker Street Muse', a typically cryptic but somewhat bitter saga of sexual and musical tribulation."

Anderson was quoted in *Melody Maker* in September 1975; "It's not intent on my part to be successful. It's just the way I'm thinking at the moment. I can just see it happening. We've had a couple of years when either people have not been willing to get into the music or I haven't been writing music that has appealed to an awful lot of people, at least on this side of the Atlantic. I'm annoyed when someone says to me that I'm going back to previous ways of thinking. It has fuck all to do with going back. It's just that the next bunch of songs happen to sound like that. It's merely coincidental."

"People will say that Tull is safe again and will know that they will like the songs even before they've heard them. It's just the way I am. I can relate to myself, I can see myself going on *Top Of The Pops* or something and going on and being a bit naughty and the producer being on the verge of saying: 'Cut, cut, you can't do that. This is a family show' — I can see myself doing and getting into naughty things. I can get into doing that again so I might just do it. I might just write a song to do *Top Of The Pops* with. I actually think I would enjoy doing it at this point in time."

"Two years ago I didn't want to do anything. I didn't want to do a single or anything like that. I was into playing the music or doing shows. It was on a different sort of level. Maybe it's something that happens to you when you start getting near thirty. Maybe it's as simple as that... It's coincidental also or contemporaneous, if you'll forgive the word, with a rebellious trend against the showbiz glitter that I've been responsible for the last three or four years, along with Elton John and half a dozen others."

"We were all getting into that heavy showbiz thing. I am now getting out of it. I'm leaving all that stuff behind. I'm not into that showbiz thing any more... I can see myself taking whole new directions in the next couple of years, being like what I thought the Rolling Stones were about when I was fifteen, a real bunch of bastards. Obviously they're not the kind of blokes that beat you up in the street because they are only thin blokes, my height or a little bit smaller. Not heavy, but real little shits. No one is like that now. No one is into that level of identification any longer. Truck drivers just look at Elton John and think 'Funny clown, but I sing his songs from Newcastle down to London', but they would like to have beaten up the Rolling Stones."

Minstrel In The Gallery emerged to be the last album that would feature Jeffrey Hammond on bass. In late 1975, former Carmen bass player, John Glascock, was recruited to fill his shoes. With *Minstrel In The Gallery* being Jeffrey Hammond's swan song, the album signifies not only an interesting change of direction for Jethro Tull as a name but in terms of the personnel behind the name.

It was in December 1975 that Jeffrey Hammond left the line-up. He had decided that he wanted to embrace his passions and talents as a painter. John Glascock was already known to Jethro Tull and was recruited quickly due to the fact that Carmen had already opened some shows for Jethro Tull earlier in the year. It was reported in *Melody Maker* in December 1975; "Jethro Tull's Jeffrey Hammond-Hammond has left the band to return to painting and his place has been taken by American bass-player John Glascock. Hammond-Hammond joined the band in 1971 in time to appear on *Aqualung*. He has, according to record company Chrysalis, retired from music completely. 'It's not a question of Tull splitting or anything like that', said a spokesman, 'It's merely that Jeffrey wished to return to what was in effect his original interest.' Meanwhile, Tull are rehearsing in Switzerland with their new bass player and are planning an album for release in May."

Minstrel In The Gallery isn't necessarily ground breaking. Like many prog rock acts during the seventies, Jethro Tull were putting out an average of a new album every year. At the time, there was possibly a sense of it being business as usual. With hindsight though, 1975 was an interesting year for prog rock. Whilst some bands were doing pretty comfortably (Pink Floyd's *Wish You Were Here* springs to mind), a lot of other acts were either reaching breaking point or had already got there. King Crimson had called it a day (for the time being) and Yes were on a break. The Moody Blues, Curved Air and Emerson, Lake & Palmer had all been so successful in the early seventies that they were no longer riding the high waves that they once were. Punk wasn't quite yet on the horizon but certainly, perhaps with the exception of Pink Floyd, prog rock wasn't on the steady footing that it had previously been. It is with such hindsight that, looking at where Jethro Tull were at with things by 1975, maybe things weren't so bad for them after all.

Musically and commercially, *Minstrel In The Gallery* made its mark then and it is still memorable today. That's not to say, "well done Jethro Tull, at least you made an album when other bands didn't". What I'm getting at is that even with the odds against prog rock at the time, *Minstrel In The Gallery* is, in some ways, an album that showed that Jethro Tull still had a lot going for them at a time when other prog rock bands were either floundering, on a break, or broken.

Martin Barre recalled in *Zebra Butter* in April 2018; "We probably were rebels. But not in the way that punk music was a rebellion. The Sex Pistols hated prog music and punk was their message to all the pomposity. With Jethro Tull we were in an era where bands wore wide trousers and had hair down to their ankles. It was a bit silly, this sort of prog rock star era. We never wanted to be rock stars, we laughed at that. We looked at ourselves and said: 'Look, we're just musicians, we're quite ugly.' So we laughed at ourselves and we presented our music in a very different way."

In December 1975, Anderson spoke to *Circus* about the

direction he saw music going in; "What I think at the moment is — this is a crude generality and the argument is full of holes but it stands up in some way — twelve, fifteen years ago we were in the midst of a very pop oriented scene. Everything was very stylised, and what sold was of a very limited musical nature. It was simple music, very technique written: the techniques weren't so advanced production-wise and recording-wise as they are now, but nonetheless they were well-tried, well-executed techniques. To wit: all those early rock and roll records with their echo effect, multi-tracked tambourines — the Phil Spector sound. Very naive music and naive lyrics but very catchy because everyone could relate to them."

"Most of these rock groups had their origins in the pop music a few years before — Ritchie Blackmore, Jimmy Page, all those, guys played on pop sessions. Keith Emerson used to play in a soul group, Jon Anderson from Yes used to play in a group called the Warriors that used to play top twenty hits. We used to play blues and soul music hits of the day when we were semi-pro. We went through that formula kind of music and then we went through this period where some of the artists started writing their own music, with 'Mack The Knife' and so on actually getting into the charts."

"Progressive rock music as opposed to the pop music of before — songs that they'd written themselves, arranged themselves, totally free from the stranglehold of the record company moulding their career and their repertoire. And the audience was the audience who had grown up listening to early rock and roll, who then went on to listen to these groups as they became more sophisticated. And now they're the rather more adult audience of today. But now a lot of that audience are getting almost as old as the members of the groups so they're not so likely to go to rock concerts, not so likely to rush out and buy the new record the day it's released. Their place is being taken by the new generation of younger kids, the new thirteen, fourteen, fifteen year-olds who have created a demand for simpler, more immediate music. Which is again a slicker, more production-ridden gimmicky version of the early rock and roll."

"That is what is hugely popular now in England. This simple sort of bubblegum rock is what has taken over — and those records sell more than Led Zeppelin sell, more than the Rolling Stones sell, more than Pink Floyd sells, more than Jethro Tull sells. England had T. Rex, now it has the Bay City Rollers, Mud, Slade, all kinds of names. When this contemporary young audience in two or three years is bored with this elemental rock and roll, then when it gets of a drinking age it will find itself in the clubs and pubs and will breed a new cycle of club underground groups. Out of that will come the new Pink Floyds and Jethro Tulls."

So why was the popularity of prog rock waning by the mid seventies? Well, from an audience perspective, perhaps people were bored of it by then. Besides, all trends change because that's the very nature of them. Also though, from the perspective of the people responsible for making the music, it is plausible that the tried and tested vehicle of prog rock was no longer fresh and exciting enough to inspire new creative input. How ironic that the very source of inspiration had now perhaps become a ball and chain of tedium! A bit too same old, same old. Equally, a cynicism towards prog rock had been emerging for quite a while. There are countless sources where bands, fans and the media touched upon the idea that prog rock was pompous and self indulgent and, after its hey day, was no longer worthy of the same attention and admiration. Put bluntly, it is possible that many people had run out of patience with it.

Around this time, perhaps Jethro Tull were ironically lucky. I'm not saying this to get a laugh but really, were they ever that fashionable? It could be considered that being quirky is a good way to protect yourself from the comings and goings of different trends; if you're always outside of what's fashionable then philosophically, that's probably quite empowering. Keeping their heads down, getting on with it and creating *Minstrel In The Gallery* was probably a good bet for Jethro Tull in 1975.

Anderson told *Sounds* in January 1976; "It gets harder and harder as the years go on but not quite so hard for us as some groups. Our audience allows us to change. They almost expect something different. Some groups are expected to remain faithful to a certain niche in rock. Jethro Tull is allowed to change. I think I was more inspired on *Minstrel In The Gallery* but in all fairness to the group I don't think they were." To which David Palmer added; "If you look closely at *Minstrel In The Gallery* you'll find that it's nearly all Ian."

As with Jethro Tull's earlier albums, *Minstrel In The Gallery* features a fair bit of Ian Anderson's observations of society and his feelings towards it, expressed through clever lyrics carried forward with expressive delivery. Whilst it certainly isn't my place or intention to take a wild guess at what any particular lyric of his means, there is certainly a lot to be said for the story of *Minstrel In The Gallery* in terms of what was going on in Anderson's life at the time.

For instance, *Thick As A Brick* had lyrics inspired by adolescent angst, penned by Anderson's fictional schoolboy character, Gerald Bostock. By the time of *Minstrel In The Gallery*, an amount of the album's content was inspired by frustrations that Anderson had as a famous adult who was touring the world and coming face to face with the annoyances relating to that. It comes across that a lot of the inspiration behind Anderson's work has been fuelled by some kind of frustrated passion to question his environment.

As he told *Sounds* in January 1976; "The problem with school is you are taught how to arrive at trite results, it's just blechhhh. My parents wanted to send me to university, send me out to be a doctor, dentist, lawyer or teacher. I'll probably make the same mistake as my father but trust that my son has enough grit and common sense to say 'fuck you dad I'm gonna do what I want to do'. Now my parents say 'well we did what we thought was right at the time' — They're probably right. If they hadn't been officious and narrow-minded I might not have had the incentive or the desperate desire to prove myself in a field completely outside their normality."

Minstrel In The Gallery was certified gold in both the UK and the US. It reached number twenty in the UK and number seven in the US. The album also fared well in Norway, Denmark and Austria where it reached the top twenty in each country.

At the time of writing this book, it is Jethro Tull's ninth best selling album. However, *Minstrel In The Gallery* was given some extremely mixed reviews from the press at the time. It adds to the interest of the album because the extremes to which it divided opinion (and probably still does) is fascinating.

Rolling Stone reviewed *Minstrel In The Gallery* in November 1975; "Chances are, most of you have long since forgotten the notion of Elizabethan boogie as an art form. Well, it's revived here on *Minstrel In The Gallery*, Jethro Tull's latest concept-as-afterthought entry in the fall record sweepstakes. The fact that Ian Anderson and the lads have once again plundered the British secular music tradition signifies little and delivers less."

"Anderson, still holding to a self-consciously bizarre musical stance, has difficulty maintaining the centre of attention with his mannered vocals, irrepressible flute and acoustic guitar. And although, accompanied only by his guitar, he introduces each hauntingly familiar refrain as a ballad — aided by intimate spoken intros and incidental studio background noises — the tunes are soon deluged by a wash of lugubrious string passages and the anachronisms of Jeffrey Hammond-Hammond's mechanical bass lines and Martin Barre's hysterical electric guitar montages. In addition, contrary to the LP's basic concept, the lyrics are instantly forgettable. In keeping with the times, Tull does get points for technical competence. Still, despite the diligence with which these gents execute the often clichéd arrangements, the most soulful moment on the album is a line from 'Baker Street Muse', sung in passing by Anderson as he leaves the studio. Finding the door locked, he screams: 'I can't get out!' That's roughly the same feeling that this listener got about midway through side one."

When *Minstrel In The Gallery* was released in September 1975, commercially, Jethro Tull still had everything to play for but of course, the band had a relatively long-standing legacy by then and it is plausible that the pressure could have been on. As was advocated in *Melody Maker* in September 1975; "It's 1968 and Jethro Tull, four weirdos led by an even stranger geezer in an oversize army surplus coat, have just made the big time. Can they get any bigger? By 1975 Jethro Tull believe that they have, and they will. Despite the notable success of the past, Anderson sees Tull reaching younger audiences."

Anderson was quoted in the same feature; "From a very personal point of view, I want to continue to justify the place on my passport which says 'occupation: musician'. I feel that I've not yet really justified that. I am not fully and wholly a musician. In some sort of deep, metaphysical way, I'm not yet that. I would like to be remembered as being a musician. I would like to be seen in history as a musician, circa mid-twentieth century. That would do me fine. I merely wish to continue that self-justification of the term 'musician'. It's what I do. It's my job. It's my living. A few times I feel that I'm nearly there but the only thing that ever concerns me is the next record or the next tour. I'm always excited about the future. I'm probably one of the few musicians you'll ever meet who isn't jaded about music. I get depressed but I don't get jaded. Since '69 I've never considered giving music up. I often consider doing it in a different way. I often consider going to the BBC and writing music for David Attenborough travel films when I get really pessimistic about my own stuff. I never want to leave playing music. I don't have something else lurking in my mind that I'd like to do, other than being a Formula One racing driver. But that's what I want to do when I grow up."

Minstrel In The Gallery showcases high quality compositions and excellent musicianship from all band members; complex yet memorable songs are played with precision and power. With Ian Anderson's lyrics being those of an emotional artist who, in some ways, probably wanted to stick two fingers up to the music media at the time, the album is full of conviction and character.

Thick As A Brick featured a sense of humour that was cheeky and by the group's own admission, Pythonesque. *A Passion Play* was thematically darker whilst continuing with the long song format that had been established in *Thick As A Brick*. It was with *War Child* that Jethro Tull went back to a more typical, shorter song format. By 1975 however, the humour and content of *Minstrel In The Gallery*, to an extent, is very candid and in parts, possibly a bit of a "fuck you" aimed at several sources of Ian Anderson's frustration. Good. If that is what happens to be the cause of great music, then *Minstrel In The Gallery* is an album worthy of further exploration.

Chapter Two

The Making Of Minstrel
In The Gallery

Ian Anderson, Martin Barre (guitars), John Evans (keyboards), Jeffrey Hammond (bass) and Barriemore Barlow had done close to five years as a touring band by the time it came to making *Minstrel In The Gallery*. With recording albums taken into account, breaks in between such times had been minimal. Whilst this line-up of Jethro Tull had been stable for five years, by 1975, there were tensions present.

Barriemore Barlow recalled in *Penny Black Music* in April 2014; "We did non-stop world tours, about a dozen albums — an exhausting time. Very physical, too. You had to be as fit as a butcher's dog. I'd lose twenty-five pounds and drop to under eight stones — that's about fifty kilos for the benefit of your younger readers — by the end of a tour. But the first five or six years were fantastic."

Jeffrey Hammond told the *Blackpool Gazette* in January 2018; "It was really exciting touring the world and I enjoyed it for five years, but I couldn't see myself making a career of the music and inside I knew I wanted to paint."

After a fifteen-month absence from the American touring circuit, the band embarked on a gruelling two month tour at the beginning of 1975. In an interview with BBC Radio in 1979, Anderson said; "That was a long tour that we did, around the time of the *War Child* release, made all the longer because we had four ladies playing three violins and a cello on stage with us every night. We rather liked the idea of four ladies dressed up in evening gowns and long blonde wigs, an actual chamber music quartet on stage, and they had their own little solo spot. It was in fact quite fun. They found it very technically difficult to play with the group on stage because we tend to play at a rather loud volume, and I had all their violins fitted with pick-ups so they could be put through amplifiers so they could at least hold their own."

"It worked quite well, but I think after their two months on the road and of course the associated tours in Europe and England and soon, at the end of the year they were all perilously close to nervous breakdowns. In fact one or two of them actually had them. It's understandable I suppose — they were all from the classical tradition and played with orchestras, and they came along to this audition for a bit of a laugh, to do a rock group tour, and found themselves involved in it perhaps in a way that they didn't expect to become involved. I mean they did become part of the touring ensemble: they travelled with the group, ate with the group, but (with a few exceptions) didn't sleep with the group. Anyway it all got really difficult because we completely forgot that they all had periods and things like that which made them rather difficult, and they all managed to have them staggered at different times throughout the month so never a week went by without one of them being in a foul mood or breaking a violin or hitting the roadies or something. So they struggled manfully — ha ha, no pun intended — they struggled through it all and they did very well, all things considered."

Ian Anderson was responsible for the production on *Minstrel In The Gallery* whilst Robin Black did the engineering. Twenty-four-track recording equipment was used to make the album. It was housed in a truck that was parked outside the radio station that the band used to rehearse in. Some takes for the album were performed in an actual gallery (as is documented on a photo on the record's back cover).

In an interview with BBC Radio in 1979, Anderson said of *Minstrel In The Gallery*'s title track; "The title track came up because the studio we worked in there had, as evidenced from the photo on the back cover, a sort of gallery part, a second level higher up at the back which is where we in fact made the album. We didn't occupy the greater part of the studio, but simply used it as storage and for making cups of tea and playing badminton. The actual recording was done up on this balcony area, although in comparatively modern architectural terms it did represent a hall with a gallery where musicians did in fact carry out their day's work. The title song — I can't remember when or where I wrote it — certainly fitted in with all of that and became the title of the album, simply from the way in which we made it. That's why we're all standing up there, you see, being minstrels in the gallery. The front picture of course is the historical version of the same idea."

The title of the album makes reference to the gallery space that features in the likes of castles and manor houses. Such is the imagery on the album's cover. The album's cover art is by Ron Kriss and Joe Garnett. It is based on a print by Joseph Nash. The minstrel analogy is alluded to in the words spoken at the beginning of the songs, 'Cold Wind To Valhalla' and 'Baker Street Muse'. It is incredibly varied stylistically. Hard rock blends with long instrumental passages that feature elements of acoustic folk music.

Minstrel In The Gallery was the first Jethro Tull album to be recorded with a mobile studio. Up to that point, all Jethro Tull's albums had been recorded in London, but in early 1975 the band purchased their own mobile studio named Maison Rouge. In an interview with BBC Radio in 1979, Anderson said; "We'd been recording in England all of the time apart from the time we spent in Paris doing the album that didn't turn out to be *Passion Play* that was aborted and re-recorded back in England, but we'd often expressed certain misgivings about the English studios and thought that it would be nice to have a mobile studio environment where we could go and record at any time, including the possibility of recording live shows or whatever else. We were advised by our accountants that it would be a good idea to put some money into building a studio, thereby saving ourselves the continual studio bills that we pay every year to other people, allowing them to make a profit. We would also have the freedom to go anywhere else to work, which had certain beneficial tax implications, I won't pretend otherwise."

"We couldn't record in America, and we never have recorded in America apart from something that was recorded a long time ago in Carnegie Hall, because in America you have big union problems, and we have a problem there with the Inland Revenue because if we record there we will end up paying all of the tax to the Americans and then have to try and convince the British that we don't owe them the money as well. So America's always been out for us, to record in."

"We took it over to Monte Carlo, basically because through a friend of a friend we found out there was a studio, an old Monte Carlo radio station, an old-fashioned orchestral studio, which was free and empty. It had no equipment to go with it; it was just a big empty room, acoustically quite good for recording. It had a car park next to it where we could park the truck, plus lots of hotels, and in the cheap out-of-season rate we could get everywhere it made it economically viable to go there and do the work."

"So we went there and rehearsed, and the truck came over and we made the album there. Basically it was a move to get away from what was becoming a bit of a yearly event: going into a British studio at a certain time of the year and trundling out another album. The mechanics or recording, the actual going from home to the studio in minicabs or whatever else, all of that was just getting a bit like something you did every year at a certain point in time. Going to Monte Carlo, theoretically anyway, was a nice change for everybody."

In Australian *Go Set* in August 1974, the reporter introduced the subject of money; "We then got down to the money world and its relation to the band. The money world incorporates the record companies which Ian refers to as 'they'." To which Anderson explained; "The rest of the material we recorded will make it one day on some level as a record, as 'they' refer to it in the marketplace of the business, which is not bad really. I'm not poking fun at the marketplace, or 'they' for that matter. All that is really very necessary, in fact one of the things I have to be reminded of frequently is my responsibility to myself in disposing of my extremely ill-gotten gains in the most advantageous way for myself and ultimately my country."

"Since to do the wrong thing means disposing of it in not the most advantageous way for either — paying vast amounts of income tax to be dispersed as half a bottle of milk to some screaming infant in Bradford, or as a few precious molecules of Uranium 237 in the warhead of some borrowed atomic powered American missile. Neither of those are ways in which I'd like to use my money. I don't quite know what I'd like to use it for, but I'd like to have the freedom to do something with it which would be of some use. I feel that obligation. In fact, that was one of the things we found out last month when we got down to working out how much we were worth and horrifically finding out that we weren't actually worth anything at all because we couldn't actually get the money we'd made. It wasn't actually ours, it belonged to various companies. The whole thing is very weird — you find yourself coming down to the situation where you're working for a weekly wage, just like anybody else, and it doesn't amount to that much more than the national average."

Recording began not long after Ian Anderson's divorce from his wife, Jennie Franks (a photographer and actress, she was actively involved in writing the lyrics on *Aqualung*). Whilst the songs on *Minstrel In The Gallery* don't seem to reference lost love in a way that is prominent (it certainly doesn't seem to be a key theme), there is certainly a strong reference to a range of emotions on the album. As Anderson sings, the minstrel "brewed a song of love and hatred."

Anderson recalled to *Guitar World* in September 1999; "*Minstrel* is one of two albums that were made during the year we recorded abroad to avoid the UK's exorbitant tax rate on performing artists. Both *Minstrel* and its follow up, *Too Old To Rock 'n' Roll*, were made in Monte Carlo and in the same year, although they were released in different years. *Minstrel* is actually a reflective album, because lot of the music on it was written at a time when I was looking back with some nostalgia on my life in the UK. I'd always lived there and suddenly I was out for a year. So a lot of the songs — like 'Baker Street Muse' and the title track — are reflective of London city life. The music also reflects my life as a musician since at that time I was not in a permanent relationship and living out of a suitcase, hotel rooms and rented apartments."

Anderson was quoted in *Louder* in August 2019; "I suppose I was feeling a little isolated. I felt you were in the public domain, but cut off, like entertainers, minstrels, in the gallery. Separated from the people you were performing to. You were of a different caste. You were travelling salesmen, carnival people. So they found you seductive and interesting, and wanted to receive your entertainment, but you didn't belong with them. Some enjoyed living in the rock 'n' roll world, whatever that meant, having their own separate identity. But for me it was not lonely, exactly, but I belonged nowhere."

"You had Mick Jagger trying to move among the good and the great back then, liking being fêted by royalty and the intelligentsia of the time. He flirted with that world, wanted to be accepted as an equal. I think his band mates found it quite absurd and laughed and joked about it. The rest of us just thought he was a bit of a ponce for trying to rise above his social station. And that had an impact on me. I didn't want to mix in circles like that. At the same time, I wasn't particularly drawn to the circles of my musical peers; I didn't do the clubs and the drugs and the booze, that just wasn't in me. I had great respect for fellow musicians, I just wasn't into the social side. So I felt dislocated... Feeling cut off isn't necessarily a bad thing, because it makes you resilient. It gives you a point of difference. Your goods, on the shelf, are not the same as everybody else's. And in terms of both material and musical styles, we dipped our toes in folk, classical, jazz etcetera. It's an unholy mess of clashes if you get it wrong, but if you get it right it's a delicate broth, a heady brew of flavours and tastes. You've got to believe you're getting it right. Because when you think you've got it right, you probably have."

It could be considered that the themes in *Minstrel In The Gallery* are somewhat Dickensian or Hogarthian in Anderson's descriptions of city life and freak show of eccentric characters that inhabit it; sleazy office workers, dodgy law enforcers, prostitutes and horny pygmies. To present so many grotesque characters and themes in an album is, I would suggest, a brave decision but teamed with the musical appeal of the album, why not. It makes it unique and if it serves as a vehicle of expression (as is suggested in the conviction with which Anderson delivers his lyrics), then happy days.

The compositional stage of *Minstrel In The Gallery* began in December 1974. Anderson was renting a house in California. This pattern was typical in terms of writing whilst still on tour. He told *Classic Rock* in August 2001; "We always recorded in gaps between tours. The only time we took time out to 'make records' was in 1981, which resulted in *Broadsword*."

As was reported in *Sounds* in September 1975; "*Minstrel* first took shape last Christmas when Anderson left England to pursue the solitary task of writing material for a new album, a somewhat irregular process for the singer/composer."

Anderson explained; "I left England on December 12th when everybody was getting ready for Christmas and I went away because I wanted to be on my own. I rented a house in another country and stayed there alone until January 12th and that's when I wrote most of the music. They're all the kind of songs you sing when you wake up in the morning... songs of the last year waking up in the morning. Because that's all an album ever is. I write most of the things when I'm on the road actually so it's unusual for me to go away and write specifically. It's harder to go somewhere and write specifically because it's much more of a self-conscious sort of effort. I prefer writing on the road."

Having initially set up in a radio station that had previously been used by the Nazis for propaganda broadcasts, the band now had their own mobile studio, taking inspiration from the Rolling Stones.

It was reported in *Sounds* in September 1975 that *Minstrel In The Gallery* "was recorded in Monte Carlo with the help of a special mobile recording truck Tull commissioned to be built. This resort town was chosen because it offered a suitable studio building to be used in conjunction with the mobile unit. *Minstrel* was recorded during April and May and followed much the same pattern as past Jethro recordings: three weeks rehearsal, three weeks cutting and one week final mixing. Though the album sessions flowed, there is a certain aggressiveness present in the tracks which stems not from band differences but rather from their environment."

The attractive beach environment was often a source of distraction for the band. They once constructed a badminton court out of wire and newspapers in the rehearsal space. Anderson complained in a number of interviews that the band were distracted to the detriment of the work ethic but equally, Martin Barre recalled in later years that Anderson was actively involved in the procrastination at times.

Still though, in *Sounds* in September 1975; Anderson was quoted on where he recorded *Minstrel In The Gallery*; "It drives you crazy being somewhere like that for nearly two months. It made me sick getting up in the morning and watching all these people lying on the beach with their amazing vanity. Most of them are really ugly people, physically grotesque; the women are unattractive and the men are obscene. And they lie there in the sun getting a tan to go back home to the office and say, 'Look where I've been.' And they do nothing... I get very aggressive in that sort of situation because I've got a lot of things to do. Anyway, no doubt some of that aggression came out in what I was singing about."

The circumstances in which *Minstrel In The Gallery* was recorded turned out to have a significant effect on the album. In an interview with BBC Radio in 1979, Anderson said; "The diversions of being in a famous holiday resort, even out of season, caused some of the group not to be around during all the rehearsal period or recording period, and it seemed to turn into a rather introspective album for me and had less of the group really coming through on it, which I think was perhaps a shame. Although obviously, as an album, *Minstrel In The Gallery* does have its merits and it has some good tunes on it, and it sounds to me — perhaps just because I can look back around the time when we recorded it and where we recorded it, and feel there was something lacking in terms of the group's empathy together as a musical outfit at that point in time."

"That was just the backfiring of an idea of going away somewhere with a view to getting more together, being in the same hotel and so on. But some of the guys liked sunbathing, and some of the beaches down there have young ladies on them without all of their clothes on, in fact without hardly any of their clothes on at all — so the group used to go sunbathing rather a lot. Even looking out of the hotel window with binoculars, I remember, disrupting several rehearsals. These pop stars, you know, being very frustrated with the celibacy that they lead on the road."

"It was full of industry and activity, writing songs and really working very hard. I think the others felt as though it was a holiday as well as a recording session. I'm being a bit hard on them really because they did do their best, it was just overall — there was an atmosphere which wasn't conducive to getting down to it all the time. I mean I was as bad as they were, really; we ended up playing games half of the day, silly games, playing badminton — we converted the studio into a badminton court. We didn't have a net so we used a long piece of gaffer tape, you know, the fix-all of the rock group, with copies of the imported *Sun* and *Daily Mirror* slung over them for a makeshift net. And Barrie's wife had sent him a badminton set from Harrod's all neatly boxed up as a Christmas present or birthday present or something, and we succeeded in one week in smashing all these Harrod's rackets up, much to his dismay, and we had to buy him some more. It was good fun, and it had its point as a way of working. It must have done, because we went back again with *Too Old To Rock 'n' Roll* and did the same sort of thing again, we made our next album there as well. The actual sound quality and the actual production of the album I think was really among the best that we've done. From that standpoint it was a good studio, a good environment to work in, and having the mobile set up in the way we wanted it to be we really did get a very good sound quality and a good atmosphere on the music."

Ian Anderson has often advocated in interviews that he works well on his own because he is able to just get on with it without any other distractions. Being left to his own devices during the making of *Minstrel In The Gallery* was probably advantageous to him as an artist. That's not to say that the rest of the band weren't important to the album (of course they were). It's just that creatively, the circumstances in which *Minstrel In The Gallery* was made were favourable to Anderson's preferred way of working. As much as Anderson was probably wound up at the time — post divorce and with the pressures of touring — the solitude he had during the making of the album could have easily been a helpful ingredient in facilitating constructive creativity.

The album's title track seems to mock the self indulgent culture of celebrity whilst offering some insight into how the audience interacts with such concept (I'm thinking in terms of the lyric about where the minstrel "looked down the rabbit run (etc.)…"). It was advocated in September 1975 in *Sounds*; "*Minstrel In The Gallery*, though it contains a certain belligerent feel in some tracks, is, in essence, a sensitive autobiographical portrayal of Ian Anderson. He plays the part of the minstrel and in Anderson's unique style brings the listener into his own experiences."

Anderson was quoted in the same feature; "The songs are personal songs but they're all different. It's not a concept album. 'Minstrel In The Gallery' is just all about how I'm up on stage and they're all down there and how it really amazes me that I don't alienate everybody because of what I sing about. Either they don't understand or else they're giving me the benefit of a lot of doubt. But, in the sense that we play anywhere and everywhere we are akin to the minstrels of old. If there's a gig we do it, and we get accommodations for the night and food. It's on a day-by-day living basis."

The album's title track is the only song on the album where another member of the band (Martin Barre) shares a writing credit with Ian Anderson. Co-writing credits were rare for guitarist Martin Barre. Not just in terms of *Minstrel In The Gallery* but across Jethro Tull's entire discography. Barre's heavy guitar solos had been a key part of the live material on the tour prior to the album being made. In this instance though, Barre's riff was such that it was used as part of a song on an album.

Consisting of three segments, the first is the minstrel's part of the song. A sound distinctive to Jethro Tull is there from the start; a single acoustic guitar chord followed by Anderson singing the opening line whereby his vocals are then backed by the addition of flute and percussion (similar to the beginning of *Thick As A Brick* really). The second part of the song is all about the rousing, screaming electric guitar. The rest of the band punctuate the song with a style that is typical of hard rock. Into the third section of the song and there's a memorable riff going on and whilst the verses are similar to those presented in the song's opening, the accompaniment is less acoustic and more in line with a band playing at full throttle. The title track of the album is noteworthy because it sets the mood in terms of offering some insight into the scope of what the album will cover; a healthy balance of acoustic folk styles teamed with rousing hard rock.

In an interview with *Zebra Butter* in April 2018, Martin Barre spoke about his position in the band, seemingly in Anderson's shadow, despite praise from the press for his guitar playing. "I never wanted to be a rock star or have a profile as a solo guitar player. I love playing music. And sometimes I like to stand at the back and just play rhythm, listen and enjoy anybody else play. I don't necessarily feel a need being in the spotlight. Now with my own band I get to play a lot more music, a lot more guitar, more solos. I think I become a better player just because I play more. But I just enjoy anything musically. I love the guitar. With a band in England I just play mandolin. And I enjoy it because it's different. I played huge stadiums and festivals as a rock guitar player. But sometimes I just want to be the mandolin player in a folk band, because it's just that much fun. I don't need to be adored or idolised, spotlighted. I quite like the fact that people sort of know who I am. But I'm not famous."

In an interview with *Modern Drummer* in November 1986, Barlow spoke about his working relationship with Anderson and their difference of opinion; "We had differences every single day, but it was pretty healthy. He used to let me have my way all the time. Apart from some of the tempos of things,

I played things pretty much as I felt they should be. Ian's got a ridiculous way of looking at tempos; I mean, there are certain tempos that move people, certain hidden tempos like disco tempos. He would invariably want things much slower than I would want them to be. Perhaps those tempos suited the timing, but listening back to that music, it's had its day — you know, the over-arranged pomp rock where you're struggling to hear the melody. All those bands of that ilk ran out of steam. I think, in some ways, it was easier to write a bar of 7/4 or 5/4 than to come up with a hook melody."

With regard to the supposedly clever time changes and word patterns, Anderson told *Circus* in December 1975; "I don't think it's clever, I don't think I ever kept anything I did when I set out to be clever. I have written and arranged things just to be clever but they sounded like Yes played backwards or the Mahavishnu Orchestra slowed down. But I didn't keep them, they weren't for anything, they weren't saying anything. It was just academic, an exercise."

Suitably, 'Cold Wind To Valhalla' opens with acoustic guitar and structurally, the lyrics are similar to those of the opening track, going from soft to heavy, again, showing a similar use of light and shade that Jethro Tull so effectively demonstrated in the earlier days of *Thick As A Brick*.

It was advocated in September 1975 in *Sounds*; "'Cold Wind To Valhalla' is a plaintive calling to the passing of heroes. In this moving song Anderson admits he doesn't have the courage to be a real hero but does see himself as a sort of anti-hero."

Anderson said; "It's all about why there aren't many Evel Knievels left. Valhalla was the place where all the Norse heroes went when they died. I just explain some of that in words and imagery but then go on to say that there aren't many of them left up there these days. I would dearly have loved to have gone to the moon. I can conceive of no finer thing than to have actually been the first guy off the planet. I think that would have been most enlightening. But maybe Neil Armstrong thinks the same about what I do. Maybe he wants to write a song and get up on stage at Madison Square Garden and sing it. There aren't many people like them left; there's a lot of them like me."

'Black Satin Dancer' opens with Jethro Tull's distinctive flute sound and John Evans' piano runs add so much beauty to the piece. David Palmer's use of strings is fascinating too; he could have used all manner of orchestration and yet he simply elected to go with just strings. It's not to the detriment of the piece though, far from it. The strings on 'Black Satin Dancer' add so much texture and colour to the song overall. It was advocated in September 1975 in *Sounds*; "*Minstrel* leans heavily on the relationships between people and 'Black Satin Dancer' is just such a song."

Anderson said of the track; "It's a girl's song. It's just a song recognising sensuality. It's the type of song Led Zeppelin would write if they could write lyrics. Except, in fairness to Led Zeppelin, they would have had a better riff and it would have been heavier. With my lyrics and Led Zeppelin's music we might arrive at something halfway there."

Side one closes with 'Requiem', a sweet melody peppered with melancholy. It is almost the case that 'Requiem' is a solo piece for Anderson. Only Jeffrey Hammond on acoustic bass and David Palmer's strings support Anderson's guitar and vocals. It was reported in *Sounds* in September 1975; "Anderson agrees that *Minstrel* is less of an electric album than *War Child* because the band is not playing all the time on every track. On *War Child*, all the music was written before the lyrics whereas in this case some of the words were done before the music."

Anderson said; "I had a chance to think about all the songs a lot more before we got to rehearsal. On some of them it was clearly better that they should be left unadorned with other instruments. But the electric thing is there; it's emphatic when it's there. I mean it works but there's no superfluous playing."

In *Sounds* in September 1975, it was considered of *Minstrel In The Gallery*; "The songs are all laced with the unmistakable Tull flute which takes a similar role to the one played in *Benefit*. The flute is present as a solo instrument, a solo voice, and rarely plays arranged parts; the lines are mainly improvised and set the instrumentals of the main melody line. Only in 'Requiem' does the flute play an arranged passage, another 'girl's song' (Anderson said in the same interview that 'Black Satin Dancer' was a girl's song). It began originally as a much longer piece with more verses and though Ian admits it was more effective in this form, he realised it did tend to ramble. In the end, he opted for the shorter version and used the first and last verses only. It was also one of the more difficult songs to record."

Anderson said; "Originally it was a piano song and it just didn't work. It has a particular progression in there which is sort of Bach-like played on an organ or piano — a descending bass line. It was very cold; it wasn't right. It meant doing a backing track and me singing afterwards and it just got out of hand. When the girls arrived to do the string parts I said, 'Well, since we've done the arrangement for them we might as well have another crack at it and I'll just do it once, one take, just me playing the guitar and singing. Either it'll work or it won't work.' So the next day I went in; red light on, roll the tape, and bang, that was it. A one-off thing and it came out sounding more the way it should."

'One White Duck/0₁0= Nothing At All' opens side two and it does so featuring plenty of emotion. Again the use of strings gives *Minstrel In The Gallery* its distinctive sound. *Sounds* said of the song; "There's a good bit of this electricity on 'One White Duck/0₁0= Nothing At All' — two separate songs put back-to-back because they represented the antithesis of each other. The first part is about going away and leaving. The lady begins with nothing more than the image of the free and wandering spirit; the second half speaks of a diminishing love-return situation."

Next is the phenomenal 'Baker Street Muse'. It's a fascinating track because it makes an exception to the rule of the album; it is just under seventeen minutes long. Whilst the other songs on *Minstrel In The Gallery* are of typical song length (with the exception of 'Grace', I'll get onto that in a bit), 'Baker Street Muse' offers something to the Jethro Tull fans who are in it for the long song. Commercially, whether this was a deliberate decision or not on Anderson's part, it was a good one because it resulted in *Minstrel In The Gallery* ticking more than one box on the song length front. Whilst some might find the whole long song thing a bit too long winded and a bit too prog for its own good, there will be plenty who revel in it and find excitement in engaging with all the small sections and enjoying how they connect.

It was reported in *Sounds* in September 1975; "The 'Baker Street Muse' (play on the word mews) is Ian again, this time reliving a real-life situation where he went for the woman and she 'didn't want to know. My attempts were politely refused.' He first tried to con her into it with some line, some angle ('my Baker Street ruse'), and when this fails he tried being heavy ('my Baker Street bruise'). He finally accepts himself as being nothing more than a 'Baker Street muse'."

Clearly, the track has something to do with sex — there's that 'Pig-Me And The Whore' section. I'm not going to try and decipher it though because they're not my lyrics to do that with.

Equally, there's that iconic lyric at the start of 'Baker Street Muse' where Anderson sings about Indian restaurants that curry his brain. The lyric could be as literal as it sounds or it could have some kind of deeper meaning. But it's so memorable, does the meaning matter? Melodically, it is a fascinating opening to the song because the melisma used on the word "brain" (more than one note is assigned to a one syllable word) harks back to an older style of music; very fitting for the whole imagery of the minstrel and the world around him.

And yet, Anderson is singing about an Indian restaurant. I doubt there would have been any of those next to ye olde pub back in the minstrel's day. What I'm getting at is that 'Baker Street Muse' certainly features a mix of old and new ideas and as such, the song is certainly a product of vast imagination that will get any other imagination wondering. Brilliant.

Anderson said in 2019; "I'd go and pick up a takeaway while reading some Cold War spy thriller. This was a little ritual I had after returning from a long tour to London, then writing songs for a new album. Much of it was written in that little rented cottage and on my meanderings and wanderings. Again I suppose some of the characters are not unlike some of those on *Aqualung*. You have to remember that I, like many of my peers, went to art school. So my background was in the painterly arts more than the musical ones. And the way I enjoyed pictorial art was not portraiture, and not landscapes, but people in a landscape. Almost like the cast of a play on a stage. And here the stage is a cityscape; think of L. S. Lowry, or the underrated, misunderstood Sir William Russell Flint. I'd have these characters where you leave a slight sense of incompleteness so that the audience can use their own creative powers to elaborate on your sketch. They can join the dots, put the colours in. That's what I find attractive about music: people can listen and introduce their own exploration or amplification."

'Baker Street Muse' could be regarded as an almost mini *Thick As A Brick* or mini *Passion Play*; full of prog rock ingredients — a long piece of music that sends the mind on a journey. It is clear that the song paints a picture of many fascinating characters, possibly some of which Anderson had observed whilst living in the rented cottage just off Baker Street in central London. There must have been a lot of characters there!

Anderson said of 'Baker Street Muse' in 2019; "Oh, look, sometimes you look back over your old lyrics and some of it is just toe-curlingly awful! But there are other little moments where you think: 'Oh wow. Did I write that? It's quite simple, but perceptive. For a twenty-something!' I never feel smug satisfaction, I just go: 'Phew, that was a lucky idea that came to me!' Sometimes you sit there scratching your head and not a lot comes."

'Baker Street Muse' consists of four vignettes; 'Pig-Me And The Whore', 'Nice Little Tune', 'Crash-Barrier Waltzer' and 'Mother England Reverie'. It is interesting how the track is compared so liberally to *Thick As A Brick*, purely on the basis that it is a long song because essentially, 'Baker Street Muse' has its own character, subject matter and melodies. It stands up in its own right and doesn't really need to be compared against *Thick As A Brick*. Still though, after *War Child* consisting of all shorter songs, I can see why many fans would have been happy that Jethro Tull offered a long song on *Minstrel In The Gallery* because when they did go for such song length, they did it so well.

The album concludes with the short, but meaningful, 'Grace'. As well as being an excellent ambassador for the power of the long song, Anderson advocated for how thought provoking it could be to express meaning through a much shorter song form. He told *Down Beat* in March 1976; "My big private goal, my actual composing ideal, is just to write a thirty second piece that just totally evokes something. Everyone will say, 'I know just what he means' — That's my sort of private thing. I don't get caught up in that too often, just once in awhile. There's a song on *Minstrel In The Gallery* called 'Grace'. It's just a forty second piece. I literally woke up one morning and looked out the window and just sang words that perfectly evoked for me a feeling and put it to a sort of quartet arrangement for strings. For me it evoked something that I think countless people will sort of share in and understand… 'May I buy you' is so ambiguous, whether it applies merely to the $2.50 breakfast at the airport or the whole thing. I mean, we pay for all this in one way or another. That ambiguity is a consciously put-in thing, but it's not something that anybody will really pick up on, though some people obviously will. The last line doesn't even need to be there for most people. It's there as an extra twist, an amusement. It's there if you happen to feel, like I do, a certain cynicism about all your pleasures in life. Because I wake up some mornings and the sun is shining and the birds are twittering and I feel like going out and strangling the little bastards."

Whilst 'Grace' is one of many tracks on the album that doesn't feature the whole band, there isn't a single track on *Minstrel In The Gallery* where Ian Anderson is strictly solo. At minimum, Hammond and Palmer contribute in the background. Although *Minstrel In The Gallery* is very strongly an Ian Anderson album in terms of the workload and creative input, all other musicians on the album make it very much a group effort with the talent that they brought to Jethro Tull.

Anderson said of 'Grace' in August 2019; "That song was just paying homage to the world around. It was a musical afterthought, a postscript, just thanking whatever power or spirit for the blessings that have been bestowed upon you that day. Then it asks: 'May I buy you again tomorrow?' Because in a way you pay through the nose for that good luck. So it's just saying grace, although I tend not to have these thoughts about me when I sit down to gorge myself on King Prawn vindaloo, a saag aloo, pilau rice and a plate full of poppadoms. I'm not that spiritually minded all the time. But there are moments."

Sounds considered; "A short 'Grace' closes the album in a sort of cryptic double-meaning. At the end Ian sings: 'Hello sun, etc…. May I buy you again tomorrow?', and one wonders if he's referring to you in the plural or just referring to the items mentioned."

Anderson explained; "The cynical part of me believes all of this we pay for in one way or another. It isn't free by any means. We have to put back in what we take out. I take my share of it looking out the window and you've got to put it back. You've got to pay for the next one, you've got to pay in advance."

By the mid seventies, a lot of British musicians chose to move abroad due to the tax conditions of staying in the UK. Anderson's stance on the matter was different though. Whilst *Minstrel In The Gallery* was recorded outside of the UK, it wasn't done with a view to having permanent residence in America.

Anderson told *Sounds* in May 1976; "I'm not prepared to go over to America for the sake of having an extra ten or twenty percent of my money, as opposed to paying it in tax. Ron Wood suggested he pays ninety-eight percent tax. But he couldn't pay ninety-eight percent tax if he tried. Living in Britain, Ron Wood could pay no more than about sixty-three percent. And someone should tell Robert Plant that he's wrong. It's really sad that people go around spouting this out in public, because these ridiculous figures just don't exist. You pay ninety-eight percent tax on non-earned income, but ours is earned income."

"The public believe people like me when we say we're paying ninety-eight percent tax, but it's simply not true. I would say that, overall, one can pay between seventy and seventy-five percent of all your income. Whether it's earned abroad or in Britain, whether it's from records or from concerts, you shouldn't have to pay more than that, unless you're silly enough to conduct your life that way. No way under the sun can you be paying ninety-eight percent. And it's time somebody got up and said, 'Bollocks Ron Wood. Don't give me that. I don't want to know because you're talking up your arse' — And he is. So is Robert Plant. So I have to believe that Robert Plant is saying it in a moment of fury because his favourite football team lost that weekend or something, so he's decided he hates England. Or maybe he's homesick and can't come to grips with it, so he pretends he doesn't want to live in England anyway by saying how bad it is."

"Sure, the tax is a lot of bread. But it isn't what they have you believe. That's the truth. The English people are being misinformed. They should be given the facts. People are actually starting to hate pop stars for making money and running away. Twenty-five percent of what people like me earn is still a lot of money. I earn as much as a bricklayer who works really hard. And that's a lot of money. That's about my level of income, and that's all I need to live comfortably."

It was reported in the same feature; "In an investigation into the effect of income tax on rock last year, the *Melody Maker* reported that British residents in the top tax bracket — that is, someone who lives here for more than three months a year and who earns over £20,000 — pays eighty-three percent income tax after the normal tax-free allowances have been made. These tax-free allowances include having only seventy-five percent of foreign earnings taxed. On unearned income, such as investments and dividends from shares, there is a fifteen percent surcharge, giving the much quoted figure of ninety-eight percent. The list of name musicians in tax exile includes Led Zeppelin, Rod Stewart, the Rolling Stones, the Average White Band, Tom Jones and Engelbert Humperdinck."

Regarding recording in Monte Carlo, Anderson recalled in 2019; "Oh, it wasn't a bad atmosphere, it was just odd being away from the UK, where we'd made previous records. The idea was to cut ourselves off from the distractions of home and family and friends, of day-today life. Being in a residential context it would be more of a dedicated, concentrated effort. But in some ways the reverse occurred. I'd written much of the material beforehand, so many sessions didn't require the others' input, at least in the early stages. So they ended up with time on their hands, doing day trips into Switzerland or Italy. John Evan and Martin had cars and would visit ski resorts. They were the playboys of Monaco. It was okay, but Monte Carlo is a soulless, meaningless place. We were resident while we were there, for tax purposes, but what had seemed like a good idea wasn't a great one. In fact our first time there coincided with the Monaco Grand Prix, so that was tortuous — all the roads were closed off, which meant getting to the studio was tricky. I'm a fast worker, I like to get things done while I'm consumed by the energy and emotion. I don't want to hang about, I like to crack on. So while I wouldn't over-egg it, because it is still a band record, this one has a bit more of me being private, reflective, whimsical."

Anderson spoke of the band's future in February 1975 in *New Musical Express*; "Well, having just ended a five year period of playing together, we've now stopped and started another five year period of whatever. I imagine you're right, an arbitrarily lengthy period of touring. When we make a movie, it will slot into this new five-year thing, rather than being like a sudden departure from the first. From the next album onwards, we're going to be making a visual programme to go with the music. It won't be pictures of the group playing the music, it will probably be very abstract and very much the sort of thing that you can watch as many times as you can listen to it without getting bored. Our albums will continue to come out as sound albums, in stereo and quadrophonic, but there will also be a visual supplement available. I'm very interested in the possibilities of the videodisc. I'm constantly pushing at the record company to get behind this, to start getting involved. I wish they'd try and make the consumer aware that there is an incoming market, which is very real."

Although such use of technology didn't come to be used on *Minstrel In The Gallery*, it's interesting to consider that by 1975, Anderson was thinking of innovative ways to take the band in new directions. With the musical beauty that *Minstrel In The Gallery* presents in the form of just an LP, would such innovation have been necessary? Probably not.

Chapter Three

Playing Live In 1975

Once *Minstrel In The Gallery* was completed, Jethro Tull played a small number of shows in Germany and France in June and July of 1975. After this, they went on to North America where they opened in Vancouver on 24th July. The final date of the tour was in Georgia on 22nd November. By 1975, with many tours to their name already, Jethro Tull were still going strong as a live band. A performance that took place on 27th October at the Milwaukee Arena was reviewed by journalist Dominic Jacques; "Anderson is a sorcerer — whirling, twirling and bounding across the stage. As he performs, a giant rabbit casually walks past him. Nothing unusual. No need to be alarmed. Giant rabbits show up at rock concerts all the time. Tull's theatrics work well because the band doesn't fall into the trap of taking itself too seriously. There is no pretence here. Anderson has been called 'the original madman' and 'the fool to this band of tarot card musicians' — in a profession full of fools and madmen, he is the real thing."

Jethro Tull were certainly still popular as a live band throughout 1975. After the release of *Minstrel In The Gallery*, their gig dates were still highly anticipated. *RPM* reported in October 1975; "The title of the new Tull release is *Minstrel In The Gallery*, distributed by WEA Canada on Ian Anderson's Chrysalis label. At last notification, the Jethro Tull concert scheduled by Concert Productions International for Toronto's Maple Leaf Garders, October 7th should be completely sold out by curtain time. Jethro Tull is still incredible for concert viewing, even if one has to sit behind a wall of speakers, better than the Rolling Stones at any rate."

Cash Box reported in November 1975; "Ian Anderson has always been an innovator. A gifted virtuoso on both guitar and flute, certainly. An innate sense of precision within the complex patterns he weaves through his lyrics. A master of counterpoint and harmony. A proverbial court jester. A phallic fantasian in live performance. A subdued, reclusive composer not prone to excessive comment or interview. Highly analytical of life, not wishing himself to be analysed nor categorised. Enigmatic, spectacular, a theological interpreter for contemporary audiophiles."

"Beyond these obscure references, Ian is a brilliant studio producer, as evidenced by the score of sterling albums he has produced with Jethro Tull for Chrysalis Records. Jethro Tull, in addition to Anderson, features a talented aggregate of musicians, namely, Jeffrey Hammond-Hammond, Barriemore Barlow, Martin Barre, and John Evans. When, last January, Tull sold out the LA Forum for five consecutive nights, establishing a new record for that venue, Anderson seemed unmoved. For him, the primary goal is to maintain a high level of compositional and performance excellence, to make music that fits his own high criteria."

"As for interpretation, his followers are free to associate *Aqualung* or *Minstrel In The Gallery* (his newest LP release) with whatever modern analogues they wish. He simply is the poet. From *This Was*, through to *Benefit, Stand Up* and *Thick As A Brick*, Anderson has been an eloquent spokesman through his renaissance flavoured endeavours. His place on this week's *Cash Box* cover has been a long time coming and is a tribute to his own longevity and high contributions to the state of the art. Chrysalis' Terry Ellis and Chris Wright have justifiable reason to be pleased with the music Jethro Tull is making for the world."

It was reported in *Sounds* in February 1975; "'I'm nobody special, I'm nothing, I'm not a philosopher. I'm not even a writer or a musician of any note'... Ian Anderson said that. So why are the masses flocking to see the man in the huge codpiece blow on his flute?... There had been quite a few technical errors, leading to performing errors by the band and a bad feeling. No one in the ecstatically cheering audience had seemed to notice... Jethro Tull is presently taking every concert dollar in America that hasn't been spent on Led Zeppelin. In Los Angeles, Jethro announced two shows in the 20,000-seat forum. Both immediately sold out, so a third was added, then a fourth, then a fifth. And that's the story everywhere."

Anderson was quoted in the same feature; "I go up there to play for me, not for the record company lackeys, God bless them all, nor even for the audience. If it doesn't work for me, then ultimately everything I do is a real con. I have to pantomime in parrot fashion and play the whole game of what it's supposed to be... That's why I dress in silly clothes onstage. Because I enjoy the celebration, I enjoy the occasion, I enjoy the momentum of being out on a limb and standing there glowing in codpiece and multi-coloured tights and jacket and coat and all the rest of it. But at the same time, I have to say it's really silly. And I have to admit some nights just thinking, 'What in the hell am I doing here wearing all this. Do I need this to play music? Has it actually become, in another way, a sort of crutch that I employ, to get me through the night.' Because I obviously don't wear them in rehearsals or in the studio, so why do I do it onstage? It's because I enjoy dressing up to go out. And I say this sarcastically to people in the audience sometimes, 'Well, it's nice to see you all got specially dressed up for me tonight, and you're looking very nice.' And they all cheer and applaud each other in their blue denims and their shitty T-shirts. I would just love to see some girls who made themselves look pretty because they were going to sit in the front row. But that hardly ever happens."

Anderson also said; "I read and re-read all the *James Bond* books, because they fulfil a fantasy of mine. I'd like to have a gun and polish it and check the rounds in the chambers before I went out on a dangerous mission. And I'd like to pull birds, be able to play chemin de fer and drive a Bentley... I'm nobody special. I'm nothing. I'm not a philosopher. I'm not even a writer or musician of any note. I'm just Joe Blow, Mr Average. And I pick up books off airport newsagents or whatever you call them. I declare myself open only to the same available knowledge, only the written material and the ideas that are as accessible to everybody out there as they are to me. I don't have special access to any information, and any information that I do review, I necessarily do so cynically. And that's why I'm reasonably sane." Such modesty! But whatever keeps a person grounded in a whirlwind schedule of touring I suppose!

Really, even before the release (and indeed the recording) of *Minstrel In The Gallery*, 1975 was a pretty decent year for Jethro Tull as a touring band. *Cash Box* reported in March 1975; "Ian Anderson, lead singer and multi-talented instrumentalist leader of Chrysalis Record's group Jethro Tull, looked up during a recent *Cash Box* interview and said 'I'd be flattered if any of my songs were still being played one hundred years from now. That would be the ultimate success.' In the context of the group's current success (seven consecutive gold LPs and a recent tour which saw the act sell out the 15,000 seat LA forum on five successive nights) Anderson's statement might seem strange but the artist is concerned about every aspect of life and is an eloquent spokesman not just on the subject of music, but on a variety of subjects ranging from spy thrillers to electronics."

"Anderson spends much of his time concentrating on the music he writes for Jethro Tull, and is crucially involved in the presentation of said music to the public both in live concerts and on record. 'Sound is an objective phenomenon', said Anderson, 'and I've learned to produce that sound that's best for the group.' He is personally involved in checking out a given venue that the band will perform in and making sure the sound equipment and lighting facilities are as professional and accurate as Jethro Tull itself is as a performing entity. With a greatest hits LP due to be released in the next couple of months and a studio disc in the works for October (tentatively titled *Minstrel In The Gallery*), Anderson stated emphatically, 'I'm against the idea of live albums because it's unfair to attempt to recapture a musical and visual event especially for those who weren't there on the particular night or nights that such an album is recorded. Going into the studio is private and personal and it's the only way to maintain total control over the final product.' One reason for the consistency and success of the Jethro Tull tour rests on the shoulders of the key personnel that have worked steadily for Anderson and the group for the past two years. For instance, the Jethro Tull tour at this point carries forty people."

Late 1974 onwards is an interesting period in Jethro Tull's touring history because it connotes an element of the band being in quite a tentative place with the whole thing. It was reported in *Sounds* in September 1974; "In Los Angeles last weekend Ian Anderson gave the go-ahead for a full-scale return to concert appearances for Jethro Tull. Anderson was on his way back to the UK after a five-week tour of Australia, New Zealand and Japan. The tour had been arranged to allow the group to check out their own feelings about touring again. It is almost a year now since Tull announced their "indefinite retirement" from live appearances in September last year due to pressure of work, the restrictions of a constant touring schedule and not least the disappointment they felt after the strongly negative critical reaction to their *Passion Play* concert and album."

"In Los Angeles, Anderson announced that his mind had

been made up to return to live work by the warmth of the audience reaction the group had encountered and their won excitement at playing live again. Ian Anderson has confirmed that Tull will tour Britain and Europe this autumn and America in 1975. Chrysalis have booked some tentative dates, pending Anderson's approval, and further venues including a London date are being negotiated. Dates so far confirmed are: Edinburgh Usher Hall November 9, Glasgow Apollo 11, Birmingham Odeon 19 and 20, and Manchester Opera House 22. Jethro Tull have a new album, *War Child*, set for release in October. recorded in Morgan studios London, this is not the soundtrack of the film *War Child* on which the band have also been working but a new collection of ten songs by Ian Anderson including 'War Child', 'Queen And Country', 'Bungle In The Jungle', 'Third Hoorah' and 'Two Fingers'."

Had the movie idea behind *War Child* worked out, Jethro Tull may have taken a completely different direction but as it happened, touring was probably something that came more naturally to them. It's just as well really because the whole thing led to them going on to make *Minstrel In The Gallery*.

Really, *Minstrel In The Gallery* is a product of its time and where the band was at with things at that stage in their tenure. Anderson was quoted in *New Musical Express* in February 1975; "For ten months we rehearsed and recorded and simply played together for the fun of it, without really having this big thing hanging over us. We knew we'd have enough material for a group album out of that. I put a lot of work into writing a seventy-page synopsis of a screenplay, a fairly detailed thing."

The *War Child* movie never came to be though. As Anderson explained in the same feature, going on the road was the more natural option for the band; "One of the reasons we went out and did the English tour was to decide whether or not we were going to go ahead and do the movie... whether we should take another year of my life and preclude any tours or public appearances of any sort. We had to decide whether we were going to go ahead and make a movie or go back on the road. The best way to make that decision was to go ahead and see how the concerts felt. Obviously, we chose to go back out on the road."

"I enjoy touring, that's my only real motivation. I don't have many possessions these days — just a really nice suitcase and some guitars and instruments that I'm very fond of. That's it. I don't even have any money. For tax reasons, it all ends up in companies. I don't have a swimming pool or house. Well, actually I did buy a house last year, but I've never lived in it. It's empty. I put it on the market again straightaway after I bought it. I realised I didn't want to own a house or pretend that I did... (I live) in an apartment in London at the moment. But I've decided to ditch that. I'm going to stay in hotels for a year or so. I want to write some more music, and I do that better in hotels than I do in something I'm pretending is my home. There's all these constant reminders, like dirty coffee cups in the sink and ashes on the floor and you pick up the phone and ask for room service in vain. You've got to go out and eat in a restaurant, which is usually expensive and tedious. Or you have to hire someone to cook for you, which means having to establish a relationship with a servant on one hand or a mistress or wife on the other. That also makes life for me a bit complicated, because I'm totally irresponsible with women so it seems. I think they've decided that. I think they all know that now. I don't know... what the hell. Next question."

When Anderson was interviewed in the Australian *Go Set* in August 1974 he said; "It's really actually something of a relief to get back on the road, for all of us. Perhaps more so for the others than me because they went back after the last American tour with the intention of getting embroiled in domestic affairs, sorting themselves out you see. After being on the road for three years and having no permanent base for their wives, children and mopeds and the other encumbrances of life, they became a bit disillusioned with it after a month or two, whereas I went back with my suitcase, and opened it in a rented apartment."

"Having divorced myself, though not literally (yet), from my immediate new-found family ties, really being home wasn't that much different from being on the road, except that it meant working in the studio all the time. I was the one who, two days after the group had split, phoned the others up and said, 'Right, we've had our little rest, time to start up again.' But I think they were all anxious to get back on the road again. Me too."

"As soon as our recording schedule was through it was very nice to get back on the aeroplane again and do that sort of five musketeers thing, which is really nice. It's a very physical act, getting on the aeroplane going from A to B to C to D and back to A again. It's a very physical shifting of one's material body around and it takes place on stage in the same way, but there's a necessity for a physical performance, a physical expression of what essentially is just a pile of jumbled abstracts in the form of a loose verbal imagery and a cacophony of notes under which one attempts to discern some logical harmony and time signature. A very physical thing, I think that's what it's all about. You know after a while, after a few years of touring you being to equate physical moving of yourself, the travelling with the sense of day to day progression of your life. The minute you stop still and stay in one place it really feels like you've lost all your impetus, stopped moving, stopped living almost. Travel becomes very necessary after a while and becomes addictive in a certain sense. You have to continue to play a constant reaffirmation of your worth as a human being, in the most elementary way — to discern once again who you are and what you're here for: We provide a public service. I suppose it's a bit like gas and electricity. I mean, we are our own natural resources."

By 1975, Jethro Tull had an established approach to live performances as Anderson told *Melody Maker* in September 1975; "I've always been dead set against that sort of ridiculous encore syndrome that most groups, who should have known better, finally submit to. You have a group like Procol Harum playing their own particular and peculiar home-grown music, their own niche in the music world, for an hour. Then they would go offstage and the audience would bring them back on. They are being brought back on the strength of the music they'd been playing for the last hour but they come back and play some third-hand rock and roll, simply because that's the easiest way to get the audience standing up, clapping their hands and breaking a few seats. That's a ridiculous situation."

"I've always firmly believed that the encore is part of the show. It's such a predictable thing. I'm not going to go back on and play rock and roll or somebody else's music for the encore. I'm going to play some more of what we do. It's just a part of the show to me, as it is for the audience, because they know that when you go offstage for the first time that you're going to come back again and play another half hour's worth. We do a half an hour encore because it seems a damn sight better than doing another five minutes and then going off and going through this ridiculous performance of being brought out again for another five minutes."

"There are groups who delight in doing four or five encores but that's bullshit. It's bullshit because everything is calculated in terms of saying that they'll save this song for the third encore and then they find themselves on a night where the audience isn't so heavy that they've left the best numbers for the third encore and the audience didn't bring them back. Presumably then they go back and play it in the dressing room... We come on and we say that we'll go through this absurd pantomime of the encore. We were going to play it anyway."

"The encore for us is the time we go offstage, freshen

up, have a quick drink, half a ciggie and on again. It's more like an interval. After that half hour, that's about it. I want to finish it on a very brittle, anti-climactic note so that everyone is aware that this really is the end. We don't finish the encore trying to incite people to want more. We do it the other way. That's calculated if you like, but it's the opposite effect to going on to win applause and win success by playing rock and roll and saying 'put your hands together' and all that rubbish. The audience can do that if they want, you don't have to tell them. I don't have to urge anybody to clap their hands. If they do it, then it's real. If they don't, then you haven't got into that rock-and-roll-Geno-Washington-let's-all-pretend-hard-enough-then-we-will-actually-have-a-good-time. The music has got to do it, not the tricks of showbiz, which is what a lot of people — us included but not as much as people think we do — employ. We're not really a showbiz group. I, at this point in time, am adamantly against this production sort of show."

Not only did Jethro Tull have an established approach to their live performances in 1975; the same applied, at least to an extent, regarding the making of *Minstrel In The Gallery*. Anderson said; "The stage thing has gone completely the opposite way to when we first started when everybody wore casual clothes. You've got people like Elton John, Mick Jagger and Ian Anderson going on stage in clothes that are totally unbelievable. We all go on dressed up like Liberace. We're all absolutely crazy. It's a dummy thing to do because nobody identifies with that clothing. Nobody wants a suit like Elton's because to get a suit like Elton's, you'd look just as bad as he looks in it. It's just showbiz glitter and it's funny. It fits his character up to a point but it doesn't have much to do with his music because most of his music is beautifully sung and very sensitive."

"The clothes are completely at odds with that. I'm pretty well as bad as that. My clothes are really a bit contrived. I'm fed up with being contrived. This new album, *Minstrel In The Gallery*, isn't contrived. Most of the things on it are first-take things. It wasn't a big production thing. It was all very immediate, positive and personal stuff. It was very different from the last three albums, which were far more rehearsed and far more musically controlled by the rest of the group as well as by me. They had a lot more to do with the previous albums. I took all of the criticism for *Passion Play* and *Thick As A Brick* before that. They were criticised for being overplayed. But those albums were by the rest of the guys in the group as well. We arranged it together but I took the stick."

"The stage act is contrived but not as much as people would imagine. Almost everything we do stems from improvisation and if it works, it stays. If it doesn't, it doesn't appear the next night, but we don't choreograph or arrange. It's contrived in as much as you decide that you are going to open the show with a certain song and plan certain things, like talking to the audience. We're contrived because we wear special clothes on stage. I'm not fed up with it because I always look in the mirror and think that it's actually quite eye-catching and quite funny. It is a suitable costume to wear. The fact that it is a costume is less than satisfying but if I was to go onstage dressed in black, nobody would see me and it would be boring."

"I have to behave in such a way that people can derive some sort of entertainment from it but wearing clothes like mine is for a reason. Nonetheless, it is contrived and that aspect is unsatisfying. One has to do it. One has to go along with the rules to give most of the people the best possible deal most of the time. But it's not something that I relish doing. I do not enjoy having to dress up except that I have to. It doesn't displease me that much but there is always that feeling of putting on a picture postcard caricature. It's not one hundred percent real."

Cash Box reported in February 1975; "The Forum, LA — After selling out a hard to believe five concerts at the mammoth

Forum, Jethro Tull came out opening night and stunned the huge gathering of fans with their precision and highly developed sense of theatrics. Ian Anderson dashed madly about the stage waving his flute phallically and brilliantly portraying the mad musical wizard he so obviously is. It was a stellar performance and the fans screamed their appreciation every chance they got."

"Featuring a cross-section of their material and staying away from overdoing any one period of their recording history as they have been doing in recent tours while they performed *Thick As A Brick* and *Passion Play*, Tull paced the show brilliantly and performed nearly flawlessly. Their control of the very enthused crowd is merely another in a long line of achievements. Anderson, besides leading the music, performed the function of spokesman. With between song patter that linked the music thematically and also was most entertaining and comedic, the scraggly looking lead singer/acoustical guitarist/flutist twisted the emotions of the crowd into whatever shape he desired."

"The band also shared Anderson's showmanship and performed on the grand scale so that even the fan in the furthest reaches of the arena could appreciate their onstage antics. Rabbits, zebras, and other figments of Anderson's fertile imagination also had their turns in the spotlight and added a surreal element amidst the thunder of the music. Songs included were virtually a Jethro Tull greatest hits collection. Favourites were 'Aqualung', 'My God', 'Thick As A Brick', 'Wond'ring Aloud', 'Bungle In The Jungle', 'War Child', 'Bourée' and their latest single release, 'Skating Away On The Thin Ice Of The New Day'. After tumultuous ovation which included literally thousands of flickering lights that set the Forum ablaze, they came back in a wave of glory to perform 'Locomotive Breath'."

"Beyond all doubt, Jethro Tull have redeemed themselves after being severely criticised for the self indulgence of their last *Passion Play* tour. The fans at the forum were thrilled to see them back on the stage and the legend that is Jethro Tull continues to grow and grow."

One of the most noteworthy things about the above review, I think, is that it suggests that musically, Jethro Tull never really had anything to apologise for. Whilst *Passion Play* was panned by many, the band still had a strong backlog of material by such point in their tenure. Besides, it is entirely plausible that *Passion Play* suffered commercially purely because it had a hard act to follow after the success of *Thick As A Brick*.

Passion Play aside, *Cash Box*'s review of Jethro Tull's live performance in early 1975 suggests that by the time the band came to record *Minstrel In The Gallery* in April 1975, there might not have been that much for the band, and indeed Ian Anderson to be pissed off about; they were still pulling in the live crowds and their albums were still selling well. There is a strong narrative, as is implied in interviews with Anderson himself, that *Minstrel In The Gallery* is predominately a product of frustration with the media ("I have no time for *Time* magazine or *Rolling Stone*") and how the band felt they were being perceived by the public immediately post *Passion Play*. But were things really that bad? I think it's a question worth asking. Either way, even if there was a difference between the reality of the situation and how Anderson may have been feeling about things, it certainly didn't seem to do the creative process behind *Minstrel In The Gallery* any harm.

UK

Antipodes

The album was preceded by the title track released as a single, backed with a non-album track that initially surfaced again on the 1988 *20 Years Of Jethro Tull* compilation.

    The UK promo copy of the single had the release date stamped on it, as well as a larger 'A' than on the commercial copies.

    In Australia and New Zealand, although it was also released on Chrysalis (as it was across the globe), These Antipodean releases weren't in Chrysalis company sleeves but those of the song publishers

Germany

Italy

In the seventies it was common practice in the UK and USA for singles to be released in company sleeves. Most European countries however, generally released singles in much more attractive picture sleeves.

Spain

Yugoslavia

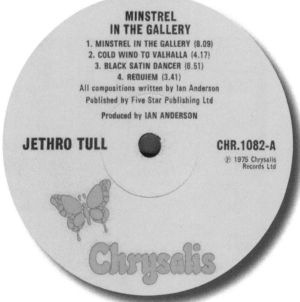

The album was released in the UK on 5th September 1975.

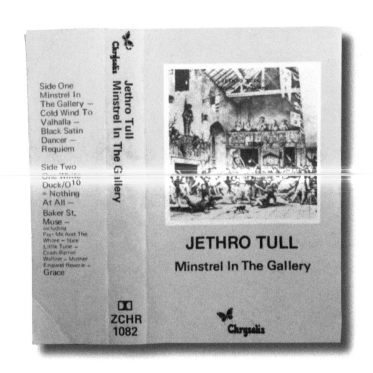

Side One
Minstrel In
The Gallery —
Cold Wind To
Valhalla —
Black Satin
Dancer —
Requiem

Side Two
One White
Duck/O^{10}
= Nothing
At All —
Baker St.
Muse —
including
Pig - Me And The
Whore — Nice
Little Tune —
Crash-Barrier
Waltzer — Mother
England Reverie —
Grace

Jethro Tull
Minstrel In The Gallery

JETHRO TULL

Minstrel In The Gallery

ZCHR
1082

Chrysalis

ZCHR 1082

Jethro Tull
One White Duck/O^{10} = Nothing At All:
Baker St. Muse: including Pig - Me And The Whore:
Nice Little Tune: Crash-Barrier Waltzer: Mother England Reverie
Grace:

Chrysalis

STEREO

Chrysalis
Records Ltd
© & ℗ 1975

100   50   0

Minstrel in The Gallery

2

It was also released in the UK on cassette.

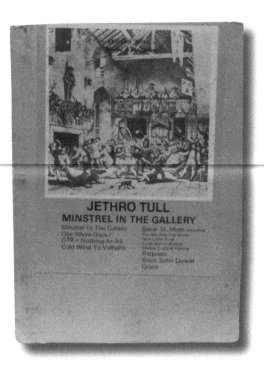

Greece

Peru

In the USA the album was also released on 8-track cartridge – a very popular medium in the States, it never really took off in the UK.

It was also released on 8-track cartridge in Italy. One of the drawbacks however, was that an album mastered and prepared for vinyl, invariably had to have the track running order changed to accommodate the vagaries of the format. The advantage? They could be played in cars!

With the advent of CD the album was first released on that format in 1983. The lettering on the cover was in red, presumably so it would stand out more.

In 2015 the multi-disc box set — remixed, remastered and with additional material, including live recordings — was released to celebrate the album's fortieth anniversary.

Chapter Four

The Legacy Lives On

Minstrel *In The Gallery* was reviewed in *Sounds* in September 1975; "A new Jethro Tull album is not the most exciting release in the world these days: not the type of record to force its way onto your turntable and remain embedded on your consciousness forever. With *Passion Play* and its schizoid time changes, Ian Anderson led his merry bunch of men through disjointed pastures, less melodic than those instantly recognisable tunes that earned the group their solid gold status. *War Child* was a step in the right direction; looking back to yesterday but leaning substantially on their 'new direction'. In concert, passion plays were interspersed with quick trips down memory lane, Anderson performing old masterpieces with a disturbing mechanical vengeance. Older fans weaned on *Stand Up* and *Benefit*, coming of age with *Aqualung*, have easily grown disappointed and disillusioned over the last few Tull years."

"That's why *Minstrel In The Gallery* is such a pleasant surprise. Quite honestly, I was dreading listening to it, expecting to see yesterday's heroes (codpiece and all) parading through the speakers, a mere shadow of former glories. But Ian Anderson, and curiously enough the band, seem on top of the situation once again. It's their best album since *Thick As A Brick* yet closer in harmonic melodies and gentle emotions to songs like 'Jeffrey Goes To Leicester Square', 'Reasons For Waiting' or 'To Cry You A Song'. The album smoothly combines the best Tull elements, wrapping them around Anderson's voice with sensitivity and understanding of the material."

"Returning to softer melodies offset by coarse sounding rock, it's the perfect working man's guide to Jethro Tull. Drummer Barriemore Barlow has stopped thrashing about at random, sticking to a more hollow sounding use of percussion reminiscent of Clive Bunker's best work with the band. Martin Barre is still not a great guitarist — one suspects he never will quite make it — but as on *Aqualung*, the lead guitar work is unimaginative but more than adequate. Bassist Jeffrey Hammond-Hammond lays low while John Evan rises to the cause with some lovely and haunting acoustic piano playing that nicely compliments the softer side of Anderson."

"The biggest change, of course, is with Anderson himself, sounding surprisingly fresh and inspired. The title track is standard fare played well with good, bitter, satirical lyrics. 'Cold Wind To Valhalla' is perfect fireside stuff, decorated by hand-clap percussions and nice in-built tensions with flute and acoustic guitar. 'Black Satin Dancer' kicks off with an introductory flute tease before the piano wraps itself around the music, ending in a merry sort of jig. 'Requiem' is another acoustic piece that finds Anderson returning to his old throwaway phrasing."

"Most of side two is taken up by the album's finest moment: four songs carefully sewn together under the name 'Baker Street Muse'. Anderson has always had both a lyrical and musical flair for concepts but this one wears better than previous forty minute epics, edited down to a rousing sixteen minutes of lovely playing. A string section supplements the band, serving as connector between harder rock and soft late night listening. With much of Anderson's material, the urban life of London lends itself to the atmosphere, the writer proclaiming himself just another 'Baker Street Muse' with Indian restaurants that curry his brain. The piece is stuffed full of his wonderfully cynical 'fuck you' attitude that made *Aqualung* so attractive.

He's even back to the gutter on 'Crash-Barrier Waltzer', while 'Mother England Reverie' is another media put-down as well as a statement on that all-consuming ninety-eight percent tax."

"Ian Anderson is quite a clever lad, aware of his ability to remain above the rock rubble. 'We're getting a bit short on heroes lately', he sings earlier in 'Cold Wind To Valhalla'. With *Minstrel In The Gallery*, Ian Anderson regains his hero stance quite nicely."

The comments about Martin Barre are so harsh in this interview! Many wouldn't hesitate to disagree with them. Still though, a positive review for *Minstrel In The Gallery*.

It was reported in the *Harrow Midweek Observer And Gazette* in December 1975; "Rarely has a musician been so bitterly criticised as Ian Anderson when Jethro Tull's *Passion Play* was unleashed in spring 1973. Both the album and the stage show got an almost unanimous thumbs down from critics worldwide. Disheartened and disillusioned, Anderson and his hand-picked band retired hurt, tails between legs, and emerged just over a year later with an album light years away from *Passion Play*."

"Yet even today, Anderson, creator of at least two rock milestones, *Aqualung* and *Stand Up*, deems *Passion Play* his greatest achievement. He says it's gripping, emotional and moving and yet, because of either critical abuse hurled at *Passion Play* or the continual battle against becoming predictable, Anderson returned to songs and simplicity for *War Child*, *Passion Play*'s successor. *War Child* was good, better than its predecessor, and even gave the band a hit single in the States with 'Bungle In The Jungle', but it wasn't the sort of stuff to put the band back up there in the higher realms of the first division."

"*Minstrel In The Gallery*, Tull's new album, is. *Minstrel In The Gallery* follows where *Aqualung* left off four years ago. Anderson is again a singer/songwriter way on top of his form, and at least fifty percent of the record ranks alongside the band's former glories. An olde English rural atmosphere permeates the album, even the band's name conjures up visions of ploughmen and farmers trekking across great fields like something out of Hardy's Wessex. A group of "strolling players" are introduced to the local dignitaries from the gallery, smattered applause, a muffled cough and a whisper and the minstrels are away. Acoustic guitar and flute crisply interweave in attractive melody before Martin Barre's spiralling guitar adds meat and grit to the proceedings."

"Anderson's singing is as distinct as ever, though it's not so much the quality of his voice which strikes home, but rather his phrasing. In much the same way as Bob Dylan and Ian Hunter, Ian Anderson embellishes verses with delicate twists of the tongue, and well-timed pauses. Just listen to 'Requiem', possibly the best and certainly the most beautiful track on the album, where he unleashes a whole host of dainty ornate knick-knacks from his box of treats. 'One White Duck/O10= Nothing At All' and a couple of sections from the 'Baker Street Muse' suite, see Anderson again as the folkie, alone with an acoustic guitar, until refreshing strings drift finely across the lyrics."

"Tull are one of the few rock bands to use strings to good effect. It all started on *Aqualung*, developed through *Thick As A Brick* and has arrived in grand style on 'Baker Street Muse'. Whether he's cavorting around with Pan's People at The Rainbow, addressing the Royal Albert Hall in green tights and codpiece, busking outside the Marquee or sticking out another Tull album, you can't really ignore Ian Anderson. He's a star."

This is a fascinating review of *Minstrel In The Gallery* because the reviewer seems to addresses the album from a standpoint that it is the band's best since *Aqualung*. A lot of Jethro Tull fans who preferred the shorter songs rather than the long song forms featured in *Thick As A Brick* and *Passion Play* may have been most inclined to see *War Child*, and indeed

Minstrel In The Gallery, as a positive direction for Jethro Tull on the basis that the band had gone back to a more conventional song length.

Of course, 'Baker Street Muse' is over sixteen minutes long but it is the exception rather than the rule on *Minstrel In The Gallery* and this is plausibly something that goes in the album's favour; it offers the best of both worlds. (Oh, and to clarify; whilst the reviewer states that Anderson considered *Passion Play* to be his best work, that isn't strictly true — Anderson has offered mixed opinions on *Passion Play* in interviews, both vintage and recent).

War Child was a very different album to *Minstrel In The Gallery*; musically, thematically and in terms of Jethro Tull getting back on their feet regarding morale after *Passion Play* was panned so liberally in the media. As much as throughout this book, I advocate for the strong motives that inspired *Minstrel In The Gallery*, that's not to say that there is an absence of that on *War Child*.

Anderson said in Australian *Go Set* in August 1974; "What *War Child* is about is aggression. It's the polarity of love and hate as opposed to the polarities of good and bad, which were *Passion Play*. It's not glorifying war or anything like that, it's just saying that within us all there is some spirit of aggression and competitiveness, whatever makes us, 'us'. Every race has this particular thing. In the heart of your heart there's this urge to live to the death, that's what it's all about. Another song which is ostensibly a love song is not really a love song. It's saying: 'War child, dance the days and dance the nights away.' It's embracing this idea and saying we have this within us, but we must use it to constructive ends. Recognise the force of it and not use it for doing the dirty on people, but use it for the furthering of the individual and mankind."

"The two things can be compatible and we must learn to make them so. That's what the album is about, using imagery, which I hope will invoke something different in everybody. I don't believe in giving people a black and white story like the cat walked in the door here and rubbed up against the thigh of the lady who picked up the head of the stuffed moose. I'm not into that bang, bang, bang clear cut stuff. I'd rather have something which is interpretive; having the sort of qualities where I, as the writer, can look back and say this isn't just a mirror of what I was then, it's something that grows, like having a shaving mirror where the colours keep changing, where you can look at it and not just see what you were but another possibility of what you were. I should imagine that the different people who listen to it, as a result of different experiences, will all have a very different way of looking at the lyrics, relating to different lines and conjuring up different emotions in relation to the individual's experiences."

As the album made before *Minstrel In The Gallery*, *War Child* is important because it signifies the point at which the decision was made to go back to making albums consisting of standard length songs. In *Go Set* in August 1974, Anderson was quoted of *War Child*; "First of all there are ten songs. It has become necessary to work in that way again for the simple reason that we have such a lot of material to play on stage. There's no way without cutting up the long pieces of music like *Passion Play* and *Thick As A Brick* (and we don't like to cut them up), to include a cross section of what you enjoy playing without extending to outrageous lengths of concerts."

"Two hours is the maximum you can play to anyone without boring them or yourselves. It's not really boring them I suppose, it's just the mental weariness. It bombards the senses to the point where they become insensitive. We could see what was going to happen if we did another long thing, which is more natural to write and more enjoyable to write. We'd get to the situation where we'd be playing the new long thing and that would take up half of the show, leaving us no time to include any of the old stuff which deserves a place in the show. It seemed best to do ten songs and pick four or five to include on stage, so we can still play the things we enjoy best from the old days. Some of those songs from the old days are still all right. To me they're like an old pair of jeans or a leather jacket, something you wear to reassert your identity. That means we go on doing those leather jackets and faded jeans, and I suppose we always will."

Anderson explained about song lengths to *New Musical Express* in February 1975; "There's so much material, so much of a backlog and so many songs that we've recorded—especially when you include the new album — that it's impossible in the two hours of a concert to play more than a bit of this and a bit of that. The last couple of years, half of the concert has been taken up with a complete piece of music like *Thick As A Brick* or *Passion Play*. If we had done another album like that, we would have been in the absurd position of playing a whole new album as a piece, then having an hour left to play what? I mean, how? It would be terrible to be so selective as to have to choose this at the expense of that, when you would really like to do both. We're in the situation now of playing ten minute bits from *Passion Play* and *Thick As A Brick*. That doesn't have nearly as much excitement as it did when we performed the entire piece. It's very unsatisfactory to play ten-minute shreds. It would be unbearable to think we would have had to hack yet another album to bits only a year after it had been done. So we came back to working on a loose concept, but with individual songs that would stand on their own. A year or two from now we'll be able to play parts from this new album and they're going to sound whole in themselves."

Musically, *Minstrel In The Gallery* was a culmination of everything that Jethro Tull had done up to that point. The album features heavy riffs and complex instrumental passages as well as gentle acoustic folk sounds, standard length songs as well as one long epic. As well as the tried and tested Jethro Tull sound, *Minstrel In The Gallery* made effective use of a string section. On the 2015 reissue of the album, Anderson stated in the liner notes; "I'm sometimes surprised listening to the album just how much string music there is. But it was all very deliberate. For other albums, the arrangements for strings might have been done before I had recorded the song, but on the other hand, sometimes the song would have been recorded, and then it would be a case of sitting down to work out what sort of orchestral lines could fit in, and where. But for *Minstrel In The Gallery*, the string parts weren't just bolted on; there was always the intention that they should be a meaningful part of the finished song, and they were considered at the time of doing the basic arrangements that we recorded."

Because of the significant part played by strings, both on the *War Child* album and on tour, David Palmer found himself more deeply involved with the band than ever before. In an interview with BBC Radio in 1979, Anderson said; "He (Palmer) was co-writing the orchestral music with me, and indeed rehearsed the string players for their tour with us. It was at that point that David became much more involved with the group because he did fly out to America to rehearse them over there, and later on when a couple of them left and were replaced with a couple of others halfway through a tour he had to come out again and rehearse the slightly changed ensemble."

"He got his first taste at that point of being out of the UK and being in foreign parts — again no pun intended — actually with the group and living that sort of a life. So when we finally disbanded the string quartet and opted for playing those sort of arrangements with another keyboard instrument, David obviously was the man for the job. And since the post-*War Child* era he has been the sixth member of the group playing basically the arrangements that he adds to the group's music on record, usually using real strings, he then comes out and does that on the road."

"I know a lot of people don't like the idea of strings muscling their way into the rock format, and they can be dreadfully slushy and overly romantic, but I do have a love for acoustic instruments. I also love loud electric guitar playing and heavy drumming and bass playing, but the idea of the two being somehow successfully wed together has always and continues to appeal to me. We have stayed with that idea almost from the word go, and we've continued to use strings where we feel that it works."

RPM reviewed *Minstrel In The Gallery* in September 1975; "The Jethro Tull vocal material — Ian Anderson — moves a little to the left of front and centre for a pounding 'out front' performance by a fine lot of musicians. John Evan's piano and organ, the drums of Barriemore Barlow, bass guitar and string bass of Jeffrey Hammond and Martin Barre's lead guitar, not to mention Anderson's acoustic guitar and flute, have an important say in this production. A beautiful showcasing of this instrumental beauty all lushed up with violins, and a cello. There's probably an incredibly large audience waiting to hang this latest Jethro Tull."

Since Ian Anderson had been at the helm of making *Minstrel In The Gallery*, it might have been natural for him to start thinking about doing a solo album. This wasn't the case though (at least, not at the time anyway). As he said in an interview with BBC Radio in 1979, "I've always avoided the suggestion that I might do a solo album, really because I think whereas any other members of the group could make a solo album without it detracting from the identity of Jethro Tull, if I made a solo album I think it would be rather different. It would conflict with Jethro Tull as a group, whatever it did on stage and whatever it brought out on record; it really would detract from the Jethro Tull identity which is, I hope as people see it, it is a group, it isn't just me, and it's something I am at pains to point out. I do my part in the group, which is a certain organisational job of work, a certain inspirational job of work in terms of writing a lot of the music. But when it comes to playing, it's played by the group as a whole. I'm the singer, and I play a few other instruments, but the other guys play what they play because they're good at it; that being the case, we are very much a group and try to keep it that way."

David Palmer's work on *Minstrel In The Gallery* is an important aspect of the album. Unlike on *Thick As A Brick* where his string embellishments were used as subtle and mere punctuation, on *Minstrel In The Gallery*, he was given the scope to add strings to the extent that they added more texture and colour to the music overall because they intertwine more with what the other instruments are doing.

On *Minstrel In The Gallery*, the strings are given paragraphs rather than commas, if you will. This is most apparent on the tracks 'Requiem' and 'Baker Street Muse'. On 'Requiem', the strings seem to emphasise the whimsical and romantic elements of the song whilst on 'Baker Street Muse', they enhance the extent to which the piece is very much a full-blown suite with plenty to say.

In an interview with BBC Radio in 1979, Anderson said of 'Baker Street Muse'; "Yeah, that was a sort of suite that was written as a whole, put together as a mini-conceptual thing within the whole album which consisted of four or five or six segments of music. It related to some part of my life when I lived in a little rented mews cottage just off Baker Street, at which point I was very much alone, just sort of sitting there, and wandering about a part of town that I wasn't familiar with. I'd never lived in the centre of London before and used to spend a lot of time just wandering up and down Baker Street. I forget the material behind it, but there's some indication I was pursuing the attentions of some lady at the time, who incidentally is in fact now my wife, so there's a happy ending to every story."

As with many Jethro Tull albums, *Minstrel In The Gallery* showcases a wide variety of musical styles. Anderson said; "One of the problems on all of our albums is that we do cover quite a lot of musical ground with each album; we've always tried to make them quite a balanced selection of music. They all have one or two or three heavy songs on them, they have one or two quiet, gentle pieces, and one or two humorous pieces or whatever. They're always fairly diverse, so one of the problems we have when it comes to music-paper criticism time, that you get a reviewer who likes his Jethro Tull on the rocks, he likes it heavy and hard, and he doesn't like hearing me singing in a romantic mood or singing gentle music with violins in the background. And then you get other reviewers who like that sort of thing but don't like Jethro Tull pretending to be Led Zeppelin or whatever."

"You get all levels of criticism: people who like one thing or the other, but you don't often find people who like the broad spectrum that we do tend to play. Hopefully, stylistically, we do make it hang together, but nonetheless there are different dynamic levels, different degrees of instrumentation, different sorts of emotional wherewithal lyrically that are in there, which do make it a little too eclectic for people, which lands us in trouble. People do tend to like a couple of songs, but the rest they hate. I can understand it; it's maybe that, as a group, we have rather broader tastes in music. We like to play a bit of this and a bit of that, especially doing a two-hour show, because playing two hours of non-stop heavy rock 'n' roll would be a complete bore, and likewise playing two hours of nice acoustic music would be a complete yawn. So we do try and go for the overall dynamic range, and perhaps it is a mistake to feel that we also have to put it into a forty-minute record; maybe a forty-minute record is not like that. Maybe we should be a bit more wholehearted with our musical approach on record, I don't know."

Anderson recalled in August 2019; "I'm well aware of the pomposity and arrogance that some see in a progressive approach, in a concept album, I fully understand all that, I get it. On the other hand, to constrain myself to only working within the bounds of obvious, conventional, catchy music would frustrate and thwart me. You have to let loose. For some that might be just turning it up to eleven, one louder. A bit more welly. For others it might be a change of direction. Or it could be an escape into the destructive world of alcohol and drugs. For me I suppose it's an unapologetic and occasionally slightly intellectual urge to push beyond the accepted norms of rock music. I'm well aware how it might come over, the reputation you might get, but you just have to bear that particular cross."

Whilst the making of *Minstrel In The Gallery* may not have been the happiest of times for Ian Anderson and indeed Jethro Tull, there is much musical merit to the album. However, at the time, it did suffer some external factors such as a lack of radio play and a few disparaging reviews. Also, material from the album wasn't used liberally during the tour that coincided with its release. Reasons for this are very much open to interpretation. It could be that Anderson and/or the band weren't too pleased with the album at the time or it could simply be the case that by 1975, Jethro Tull had a tremendous menu of music from which to choose from for their live sets.

Regarding the album's title track, Martin Barre was quoted in *Vintage Rock* in 2002; "It was done in Monte Carlo and I wrote the long intro. It was an important track, but it never really worked live. We did it a long time ago and it was very messy. It's one of those tracks everyone wants to hear, but we never play it." To this day, Martin Barre advocates that *Minstrel In The Gallery* is one of his favourite Jethro Tull albums and he holds 'Black Satin Dancer' in high regard.

In 2019, Anderson responded to comments he had made at the time of the album's release that 'Black Satin Dancer' was like Zeppelin but with better lyrics: "Ah. That was the kind of thing I unfortunately used to say, opening my mouth without stopping to think. Of course it was offensive. In that moment I forgot that Robert (Plant) wrote the lyrics. He was probably hurt. It sounded like I was claiming some kind of superiority. I was probably trying to pay a compliment to Zeppelin but it ended up not as I intended."

As a single 'Minstrel In The Gallery' placed at number seventy nine in the US in October 1975. The B-side of 'Summerday Sands' was first used on a Jethro Tull album on the 1988 compilation release, *20 Years Of Jethro Tull. Cash Box* reviewed the 'Minstrel In The Gallery' single in August 1975; "It is a far better thing that Ian Anderson has done with 'Minstrel In The Gallery' as this 4:12 is a deft return to the density and meaty substance that characterised earlier works. Lots of heavy riffing effectively compliments Anderson's vocal posturing while his unobtrusive flute runs stab at the periphery. Tull is hot this time out."

The *Cheshire Observer* stated in September 1975; "The anticipated Jethro Tull single, 'Minstrel In The Gallery', is not the blinding classic I hoped it would be. It is, in fact, a confused and noisy pop record which is only distinguished by the extraordinary voice of Ian Anderson slicing though the dirge. Maybe the album of the same name will contain more juicy cuts."

An interesting review. Everyone is entitled to their opinion and all that good stuff but if you were to imagine the single sans Anderson's vocals, does it still have a lot of distinctive Jethro Tull features? Yep! It goes beyond the structure of a basic pop song, makes interesting use of time signatures and there's plenty of flute too. Besides, as the *Liverpool Echo* advocated of the single in August 1975; "It's good to see Jethro Tull back in business again with a fine single — 'Minstrel In The Gallery'. And what a fine song it is as Tull immediately stamp their usual brand of chunky rock on an energy packed single."

Some might say that 'Minstrel In The Gallery' has a lot of renaissance era features in the music. After Anderson's spoken dialogue in which he plays two minstrel characters (followed by David Palmer's announcement of the pending performance), acoustic guitar and flute are blended with vocals and the melody sounds quite modal (think in terms of the well known 'Greensleeves' melody).

It could be argued that Anderson was aiming for a specific historic musical reference but I would advise caution against this. He was quoted in *Creem* in June 1977; "The academic delving and the subtle sharpness of traditional English music is a relatively sterile intellectual exercise... I believe first and foremost in a folk memory. I'm of particularly mixed origin; my mother is English, my father is Scottish. So you have the peculiar sort of mixture of origins in me. But I do believe in a folk memory or something which is at once Anglo-Saxon and Celtic mixed together from way back a long, long time ago and I believe that we retain something of, certainly not the academic wherewithal to put that type of music together, but something of the emotional response to that music."

It could be considered that *Minstrel In The Gallery* was one of the last Jethro Tull albums of the seventies to explore urban life through lyrics about eccentric characters in an interesting situation. It was done on *Thick As A Brick* in 1972 and it was done on *Passion Play* in 1973. After *Minstrel In The Gallery* in 1975, the 1976 *Too Old To Rock 'n' Roll: Too Young To Die* album was a story of an ageing rock star and then of course, *Songs From The Wood* in 1977 and then *Heavy Horses* from 1978 were both based on themes relating to rural life and the countryside.

In a review of Tull's 1978 album, *Heavy Horses*, it was advocated in *Melody Maker* in the April of that year; "I remember praising *Minstrel In The Gallery* to the high heavens and remarking that after a rather bleak and unproductive period Tull were back on song again."

Anderson was quoted in *Melody Maker* in September 1975; "Luckily, although we've fallen into various pits of bad criticism for various records we've done, we're always doing something different, and I think people accept that from us. The best thing there is in the world is the fact that when we bring out an album and somebody doesn't like it, it doesn't necessarily mean that they won't buy the next one. They realise by now that the next album will be something completely different and they might like it. To be a little bit unpredictable is nice."

"We don't have too much of a style. We're able to change and do different things and it seems more acceptable than it is, for example, from the Rolling Stones, because if they deviate from their style more than a little, it's just not the Stones any more. Elton John can do that as well, and he can play so many different sorts of musical styles and it still sounds like Elton John, but he's able to move musically. It's a bit more flexible than it is for the Stones. The Stones, and Zeppelin, have more of a problem because their style is very rigid. I think they must have a terrible dilemma every album time. I actually don't care. I don't go through dilemmas. I do not produce records for effect or to be successful. I really couldn't care less because, by the time the records come out, they cease to mean anything to me. It doesn't really worry me."

When *Minstrel In The Gallery* was released, Anderson still had plenty of ambition to keep exploring his craft as a musician. He told *Melody Maker* in September 1975; "I've not yet written the songs that I want to write. It comes down to songs. I'm a believer in absolute value with songs. I would like to write a really substantial love song. I would like to write a really substantial out of love song. And you should be asking me at this point what do I mean by 'substantial'? I mean truly evocative, and more than just descriptive, something that really paints a strong vivid picture. I want to write songs which portray the viciousness with which stuff from the German School of Painting grabs you. I want them to stand on their own and for me not afterwards to think: 'I wish I had done this and that.' It's not perfection. It can still have flaws in it but it still has to evoke finally the right thing. I'm more concerned with that now and I will be for the next few years rather than doing anything pyrotechnical. I'm not really into productions, big deals."

Anderson was quoted of *Minstrel In The Gallery* in the same feature; "It's very different from going backwards to *Stand Up* or *Benefit* or *Aqualung* because those were very uneconomical songs which I wrote rather badly. I wrote sparsely then. It took me a long time to say something. They had a lot of padding in the lyrics. A lot of it was just superfluous words and phrases used because they were convenient. They weren't really very good. There were some good things about them but I write much better now."

"The only thing that is difficult to continue to do is to have the same sort of raw and unrefined energy. As you develop more as a musician, it's harder to find the unrefined energy. It's easy to find that when you start to play an instrument with a brash excitement. That's the very lifeblood of all pop music — the amateurish, unrefined quality and it becomes more difficult to find as you go along. Nevertheless, I still believe that is still possible. I find it really possible when I'm just doing an acoustic number to have that raw thing. It's harder for a whole group to do it. To wit — and I don't wish to be cruel and I'm not putting them down — I sympathise with the Rolling Stones' problem of coming up with new music all the time because it's harder and harder for them to find this sort of raw Rolling Stones style as they get older. They are getting older. I'm getting older. I'm twenty-eight now, and Jagger must be thirty one or thirty two."

Upon being asked by *New Musical Express* in February 1975 if he was "tired of Jethro Tull" and "bored of the image",

Anderson replied; "I'm not exactly tired of it, but I'm not thrilled. If it's convenient for people to think of me as a one-legged flute player, then fine. I think that most people are aware that I don't stand on one leg all the time and I don't just play the flute. I play saxophone and guitar more than I play the flute. I actually find the flute a little bit tedious. It has its limitations, being a monophonic instrument. You can only play one note at a time. It becomes very pedestrian unless you're completely versed in the instrument, which I'm not. I can play well enough for people to think I'm good at it, so the object of that exercise was achieved a long time ago."

Anderson was quoted in *Melody Maker* in September 1975; "I'm probably the only one who couldn't do a solo album because if I did, it would end up being made up of all the quiet Jethro Tull songs. Would I say it's by Ian Anderson or an album of Jethro Tull's quiet songs? It wouldn't really be a solo album because a lot of the things I do with the group are solo things, at least on the records. *War Child* and *Passion Play* were much more group efforts, but the new one, *Minstrel In The Gallery*, has a lot more to do with just me. So had *Aqualung* and *Stand Up*."

"I can remember the time around the *Stand Up* era when a Jethro Tull recording session meant me getting into a taxi with a mandolin and a guitar, going into the studio, and the others weren't even there. I've done it for a long time. Whenever I do an album I get very involved with it from start to finish. The attachment that I form with it is almost paranoid. Then there comes the day when the record is actually being shipped and, at that point, it's an incredible relief because then I can disown the album. It has nothing to do with me anymore and I leave it behind emphatically at that point. I cease to care."

Throughout his career, Anderson has become known as an eccentric and entertaining flute player standing on one leg. He was quoted in *Sounds* in January 1976; "I remember proclaiming to my grandmother at the age of nine that I wanted to be an actor. She was the only one to encourage it. I suppose the idea of not wanting to grow up made me want to be an actor. Even contemporary musicians fulfil an image of their own choice and take it to its conclusion. Like Mick Jagger, or Pete Townshend, even Ian Anderson. Create an image and never grow old. All pop people have their own private fantasies but we're not actors. It's a disciplined masquerade."

Anderson's work on *Minstrel In The Gallery*, very much solidifies his reputation as an excellent acoustic guitarist (that's not to say that Jethro Tull albums pre and post *Minstrel* don't achieve this, it's just that on *Minstrel In The Gallery*, the quality of acoustic guitar — in terms of playing and effectiveness in context of the compositions as a whole — is noteworthy in proportion to the heavy rock elements of the album). Equally though, it wouldn't be balanced to state that *Minstrel In The Gallery* is predominantly an acoustic album. It isn't!

Martin Barre's contribution to the heavy rock elements of the album are noteworthy too. They certainly succeed to embellish what is going on acoustically. Essentially, every member of Jethro Tull brings their A game to *Minstrel In The Gallery* in terms of talent, even if Anderson did sound annoyed in some interviews where he stated that he had a bigger workload than the others.

As with other Jethro Tull albums, *Minstrel In The Gallery* certainly carries an autobiographical element to it. It is clear from several interviews that the album was very much a product of what was going on in Ian Anderson's life at the time, both personally and professionally. Personally due to his divorce and professionally due to the alienations he says he felt from his colleagues and peers at the time.

Anderson told *Sounds* in January 1976; "Most of what I write has some origin in my personal feelings but I also like to write about people who can't express themselves. They're all a bit about me."

Anderson's work has often been observational as well as autobiographical though. Anderson was quoted in *Louder* in January 2016 regarding one of the songs from *War Child*; "In 1974 I wrote a song called 'Skating Away On The Thin Ice Of The New Day', based on the science of the time, which suggested there was a new ice age in the offing. Later, Antarctic ice core samples started to tell us differently and we were going the other way with global heating."

In an interview with *Circus* in December 1975, Anderson was asked, "Once you've finished an album such as *Minstrel In The Gallery*, does it remain with you? Does the music become a part of you?" He replied; "After all the actual recording is finished you have to mix it, play the tapes to cut it, listen to tape lacquers and cut it again, and make changes and cut it again, and finally make test pressings — it drags it out. So it doesn't get finished really for quite a while after the music's finished; when it's actually ready to go it's nothing to do with me anymore. It's already with them, I mean they can do what they like with it. They pay $6 for the privilege. Unless I continue to play the songs onstage if they're those kind of songs that continue with me in a personal way by playing them as part of the show every night. Then I feel closer, perhaps, to the music. Not the album per se, but the music itself."

Upon the release of *Minstrel In The Gallery*, Ian Anderson explained in *Melody Maker* in September 1975 regarding Jethro Tull's personnel dynamics; "Right now I tend to be locked away from them because I'm writing material for the next album. At the moment, we don't have much to say. They're probably talking about me behind my back, wondering what I'm writing. I also have to be aware of writing something that they really want to play. There's no point in me writing something that isn't going to interest them at all... Ian Anderson is part of Jethro Tull, and Jethro Tull are a big part of Ian Anderson. That's all I do basically. I don't do anything other than Jethro Tull."

"I think that maybe the other guys have their more pertinent interests outside of the group, whereas I don't. The only thing I do is this group, which makes me more involved than they are. I do more than play on the record or play on stage. I have a wider involvement, like producing and mixing. Nonetheless, when we do get on stage, it's five people up there and I expect them to work as hard as I do and I expect them to play better than I do."

When asked if he thought the other members of Jethro Tull might like to have a more active part in the band, Anderson was quoted in the same feature; "They always can, if they want to. When Martin (Barre) writes something, as he does about once every three years, the chances are I'll use it, because the chances are I'll like it. He wrote something about a year ago which I liked. If he wrote more I'd probably use more and I'd incorporate it into the songs I was writing. He doesn't do that much but when he does it, I'm pleased to have it. Presumably, if he wanted to write more, he would. He has every encouragement to do more, as do John (Evan) and Jeffrey (Hammond-Hammond)."

"At one time or another, they have all made writing contributions. They're just not terribly prolific, let's just put it that way, whereas I am… On *Passion Play* there was a track where the royalties were split up between everybody because we were all involved. It said on it 'by Jeffrey Hammond-Hammond, John Evan and Ian Anderson' in that order. On *Thick As A Brick* there were some bits that John Evan wrote, which I don't remember he got credited for but he certainly got paid for. On *Minstrel In The Gallery* there was a bit on the title track where Martin did a three minute instrumental, which Martin wrote and he is credited for that on the album and gets paid for it as a percentage of the total royalties from the album."

"I would hate to be in the position of me having to do half and somebody else having to do half because if I didn't like their stuff, I wouldn't be able to sing it. I think, in a lot of ways, it's different being a singer than being a musician. If you're a guitarist and you don't really like the tune, you can still play it. But, if you're a singer and you don't like it, it's very hard to sing it. I'm not really a singer in the sense that I can't sing other people's songs. I honestly can't do it."

"The first year that we played in '68, which was the last time we played anybody else's songs, we changed the songs around to suit me. I could never sit down and sing 'Lucy In The Sky With Diamonds'. I would feel silly. I don't know what the hell the song's about. I'm just thinking about it now. I do not know what 'Lucy In The Sky' is about. Elton John clearly knows because he sings it with some conviction and with more than a little help from his friends. I'm less able than most people to sing other people's songs. I don't have that basic sympathy for them anyway, probably because I don't listen to them that much and probably because every time I sit down, I find myself playing the guitar with some little song of my own coming out. But I really have no idea whether what I write is a pile of garbage, whether it's okay, or whether it's as good as 'Lucy In The Sky With Diamonds'. All I know is that it takes me all my life to write what I'm writing. It's the thing I can do best. Other guys could sing my songs better. Elton John could probably sing my songs better than I can, but there are lots of other guys who couldn't. He's a very good singer and he obviously gets into what he sings. I don't like his clothes, but I think he's a good singer."

Anderson told *Louder* in August 2019; "Martin Barre and I were the loners, really, within the social infrastructure. He liked to get up early and go for a run; I liked to get up early and strum my guitar and watch the news. After a show, both of us would be tucked up and fast asleep within forty-five minutes of coming off stage! The world would be boring if everybody lived in the stereotypical rock 'n' roll way we're encouraged to believe they do. I'm sure even Jimmy Page woke up early sometimes and had a creative moment. Or it could have been a procreative moment, remembering the Polaroid photos that Jimmy used to show us the morning after the night before."

Anderson said in *New Musical Express* in February 1975; "The people that I work with day-to-day are the people that I mix with socially. I don't really have any need of much else. I don't feel the need to go out to building sites and make friends with Irishmen or anything. It doesn't seem necessary. Although if I met one in a pub, there'd be every chance that we'd get married or something, who knows. I don't have much involvement with anyone else who plays music, because I don't see them. I don't think it's very easy to make real friends with other musicians. We're all a bit paranoid. Musicians tend to be doctors for each other, psychiatrists I suppose. I know a couple of musicians, like Captain Beefheart and Roy Harper, and there's that sort of a relationship there."

"It becomes very, very heavy, very, very quickly and I don't think it does you any good in the long run. I feel a bit wary of it because we'd all end up talking about the musical desperation that we suffer from. But maybe it's only me. Obviously when you're playing music all the time you go through an awful lot of frustration in trying to create a certain sound and being unable to do it a lot of the time. I mean musicians are nice guys and all that, but we're all too much the same. Too much the same."

With Hammond's departure from the band, by the end of 1975, Jethro Tull were making preparations for their next album, *Too Old To Rock 'n' Roll: Too Young To Die*. It was reported in *New Musical Express* in December 1975; "Jethro Tull have parted with their bass player of nearly five years' standing, Jeffrey Hammond-Hammond. He has reportedly left the band to return to painting, which has always been his principal interest. Our correspondent in Switzerland, where Jethro are at present recording, says that he has been replaced in the line-up by a young American musician named John Glascock."

"Tull are in the process of recording eighteen new Ian Anderson songs, from which the best ten or twelve will be selected for inclusion on a new album, planned for May release. Anderson said in Montreux that the songs are all about people from different walks of life — an ageing rock star, a housewife, an artist, and so on. Some are sung in the first person, others in the third person. Anderson also said that there are, at present, no plans for any live dates by Tull. Hammond-Hammond played with Anderson, John Evan and Glenn Cornick in Blackpool during 1967, before Tull was born. Anderson formed Jethro the following year, but Hammond-Hammond did not join the band until early 1971, first appearing on their *Aqualung* album."

Jeffrey Hammond told *Lancashire Life* in October 2017; "That stage of my life ended abruptly. I just blurted it out at a business meeting that I was leaving with no previous intention of saying it. It wasn't the best way to handle it, but the band accepted my decision and moved on... It was fabulously exciting touring the world and I enjoyed it for five years, but inside I knew I wanted to paint — to learn to paint. And that's what I have been doing all these years. Learning."

He told the *Blackpool Gazette* in January 2018; "They were good days with Tull and I am still in touch with my ex-bandmates, including Ian, but honestly after all these years, I really don't miss playing music at all."

In anticipation of what 1976 was set to look like for Jethro Tull, Anderson said in *Melody Maker* in September 1975; "I will give you, glibly, a prediction straight off. I would suggest that Jethro Tull, in the latter half of '76, will become a much more hugely popular group. I think that, by the time the next album comes out (*Too Old To Rock 'n' Roll*) it will contain probably a number of songs which actually reach a lot of younger kids again. At the moment I am feeling very youthful and very energetic about pulling little birds and getting into fights. I'm very much into that. I'm very energetic, much more than I was a year ago, when I did a bit more sitting down and remained very calm about things. I'm a bit more up now. I don't know why."

"I don't really want to appeal to that younger audience but I think it'll happen. Just going by the songs I've been writing for the next album and the way it's going. People are actually going to think the next album really is good. People will think the next album will be really neat. The reason is that the songs, so far, will hit them long between the eyes. I'm getting better at doing that, although I don't do it all the time. It's not a style but I will employ it because I'm feeling a bit more like that than I have done for a year or so."

"The last time I was feeling super-energetic was around *Passion Play* time but then it took the form of a tremendous group thing. That's what happened. This time it's not like that. It's confined to the songs and the chords and the words and the group thing will be very carefully handled to assist that. I'm not going to let the group submerge it, the way it happened on *Passion Play*. The group will not submerge the essence of the songs, which are really simple. You will understand the words but you will also say, 'actually, that's quite neat' — I think it will be a good year."

"It'll probably appear to be the sort of music that is going to appeal more to fans that we don't have yet. It'll pick us up a lot more people who can identify with what I'm saying and what I'm doing and what I'm going to be like this time next year. I'm getting increasingly into very emotional things and I didn't used to be. It's difficult for me to figure out why. The songs will appear more directly emotional and will gain us the new fans. I think that the people who have been fans in the past will say that it's okay and say that we're back doing okay stuff again."

"One of the few ways I can retain a positive identification with the younger fans in the audience is to think that one of those kids, who is fifteen and tanked up on some drug or other, doesn't like me. He's a punk kid and I'm twenty-eight and, in some ways, a grown man, but he can still beat the shit out of me. I always think of those kids and the one way I can identify with them is to think that if he actually has a go at me in the street, I'll lay him out. That's the one thing that makes us equal. It makes me fifteen as well. Jagger looks so young. I saw him at Madison Square Garden when we were playing. He came backstage. I didn't recognise him. He was five years older than me and he really looked so young. If being in a rock group does nothing else, it keeps you young. And if you're lucky, like Jagger, it keeps you young-looking. If you're not, like me, it keeps you young at heart. It's very weird. It's a Peter Pan thing."

Do bands and their music need to have a strong youth following to be worthy of artistic acclaim and commercial success though? Not necessarily. As was reported in *The Age* in July 1974; "Jethro Tull Wins Over The Mums — Four years ago the leader of English pop group, Jethro Tull, won an award he didn't like — the pop figure most hated by parents. Things have changed and Ian Anderson, whose outrageous stage acts caused many mums to stop their daughters seeing him, claims that half of Jethro Tull audiences are made up of parents. 'Now the mothers are coming with their children', says Anderson."

There's nothing wrong with coming of age. Anyway, it could even have been something that expanded the thematic scope presented on *Minstrel In The Gallery*. As *Sounds* reported in September 1975; "Ian Anderson has just turned twenty-eight years old, a fact which pleases him none too greatly. His physical appearance belies his true age — reddish hair and beard frame his thin face and the lanky frame is rarely stationary. Though the subject of age puts a damper on his thoughts, the prospect of talking about Jethro Tull's newest album does not. Titled *Minstrel In The Gallery*, it is a far more personally reflective record than *War Child* or any previous Tull project."

In the first chapter of this book, I touched quite a bit on how it may have been to Jethro Tull's advantage that as a band, they never seemed to be about being fashionable and following trends. It strikes me that *Minstrel In The Gallery*, as with pretty much every other Jethro Tull album ever, succeeded in interesting circumstances; whilst there was a need for the band to think commercially, it comes across that Anderson was reluctant to compromise the music on such basis.

For a band making an album every year throughout the seventies, such philosophy must have required quite a balancing act. Anderson was quoted in *Cash Box* in December 1978; "One of the sad things about my job, is that in spite of the artistry to which one might subscribe, it does come back to using the same words in terms of selling the product as is applicable in any other industry, such as packaging and merchandising and 'the industry' as it's referred to. I cringe in embarrassment when I hear people talk about 'the industry'. Our business has a special flair that shouldn't be lost in the trite business aspects. I see many people who had the flair, that special creativity, who now have become concerned about maintaining that position as part of 'the industry'."

Of course, there was perhaps an element of cynicism in Ian Anderson's approach to the commercial side of music. Speaking with *Melody Maker* in September 1975 he said; "People's reactions are dulled to anything that is overtly controversial nowadays and controversy only comes from character. It has nothing to do with wearing funny clothes or adopting postures and images. People see through that too much now, so much so that they are quite willing to accept the posturing because it's so transparent that it doesn't offend, whereas five or six years ago the posturing would've offended. It no longer does.

Now it's just tinsel. There are a few people who are real, meaningful characters. Frank Sinatra is a real, meaningful character. When he opens his mouth to sing or speak, there's the weight of a tremendous character coming through there. But when somebody like David Bowie or Elton John speaks, it's inarticulate and blundering. My money's on Frank Sinatra to be around in ten years time."

Anderson continued in the same feature; "You still have those names from five to ten years ago: the Stones and Zeppelin, the Who and Elton John. Those people still sell records. Competition as such, though, never seems to affect us. It would only affect us if we brought out an album at the same time as Led Zeppelin and the Stones. The Stones, actually, would probably come off worse. It's a terrible thing to say but their record reputation is possibly less than ours, although their live concert reputation is correspondingly greater."

"If you put three major groups on the road together, one of them would suffer. I can see it coming that, economically, the concert business is going to take a turn for the worse everywhere. It might happen to us. When the costs of our overheads continue to escalate, and inflation is rampant, our ticket prices do not reflect inflation and our increased running costs, so therefore our profit margin is reduced. If one pursues that trend, there clearly is a time when we can no longer make the same kind of money. We have to put up ticket prices. It makes people less likely to go because they have less money than they ever had… for a long time, what it cost to go and see a gig, whether it's by Joe Bloggs at the Marquee or a cheap seat at the Albert Hall, one could equate it with the cost of a cheap meal. The most expensive tickets that we sell are the cost of an average-priced meal. I draw the line. I can't bring myself to charge anyone more money than they would spend for an equivalent time eating in a reasonable restaurant."

"That's about as far as it goes. As soon as it costs more

to go and see entertainment than it costs to fill your belly, it's not worth it any more. Look at Frank Sinatra and the prices he was charging for his concerts, and he bombed out everywhere. People just will not pay that sort of money! The people who are willing to pay £30 and £40 for a meal are very few and far between... Our audience does not go to the Ritz, and our music is not equivalent to the food in the Ritz. We give a good hamburger's worth. That's all. I'm being really honest. What I do on stage is a good hamburger number. What Mick Jagger does on stage is maybe worth two hamburgers. Let's be honest. What's more important? Seeing somebody cavort about on a stage singing a few songs he wrote in a bedroom somewhere or getting a good meal inside you? It's down to filling your belly's worth and no more. It's the same with albums. An album is not worth more than the cost of taking your bird out for a night to the cinema in London. It should cost about the same. I'm aware of it in those simple terms. That's probably how the guy in the street thinks about it. That's how he subconsciously equates it."

Ian Anderson clearly put a lot of thought into what he needed to do in terms of showmanship and giving an audience a good experience. He was quoted in *New Musical Express* in February 1975; "We are totally incapable of playing something that we don't like. To play a song or a style of music that we did not enjoy would be an act of prostitution. So far there's been a lucky coincidence that the songs we like doing are the songs people like listening to. I'm glad the older songs that we play on stage now tend to be the ones that the people want most to hear. Which just goes to show that they all have a very good taste."

"If I had to worry about maintaining my success, it would be very uncomfortable. That's why I live week-to-week. I don't worry about selling a million records or selling out tours. I just think about making records that appeal to me. That's enough... What we do at the end of a show is very important. If we were to build the momentum up to a frenzied peak and then split, the kids are gonna break a window or punch a policeman. I always like to take it downright at the end so that it's a very anti-climactic point to finish on and there's no way that you can come on after that and do any more. The audience knows that. So when we play an encore and it lasts thirty-five minutes, that is the end and there is no way that there could be any more. That is it. So you can throw the house lights on and stop the clapping straightaway. Everyone leaves the theatre quietly with a good, calm feeling."

It was advocated of *Too Old To Rock 'n' Roll: Too Young To Die* in the *Liverpool Echo* in May 1976; "Jethro are a strange band. They have produced some brilliant stuff in the past and now seem stuck in a rock rut. Possibly the effect that Ian Anderson was after on this album but following *Minstrel In The Gallery*, I had hoped for better."

Minstrel In The Gallery had certainly made its mark. It fascinates me to wonder if perhaps in some ways, the album meant more to the fans by the late seventies. Anderson was quoted in *Cash Box* in December 1978; "Ten years of playing on the road is a massive achievement. In our case, it marked a suitable point for reiteration, for perhaps making a definitive recording of songs that have remained as stage performances a good many years. Things that are cyclical, such as making an album or doing a tour, are best done unbroken. To me, the cycle of getting off the plane, going to the hotel, doing the show, and getting back on the plane is a very important part of touring. That's why I don't like to do more than one night in a city, it breaks the cycle. That's also why I don't like to listen to our earlier albums, because I'm already in the cycle of the next album and I don't want to break the cycles. Once the mixing is done I even have a great deal of difficulty listening to the test pressing. It becomes a painful process, inevitably one hears something that could have been done better. I prefer to leave serious examination of my work to the people who buy it and listen to it. There's an essential difference between the performer and the audience and you can't pretend they're doing the same thing."

It is plausible that Anderson's cynicism about the music business around the time that *Minstrel In The Gallery* was released was something that went on to inspire *Too Old To Rock 'n' Roll: Too Young To Die*. Anderson said in 1975; "I think it's all become very showbizzy again. Particularly in England, it's very much back to the two or three-hit wonder situation. We're back to the days of early rock and roll again. I don't think it's so bad, but I think it obviously makes for rather temporary values, which is not a good thing for kids who are growing up and learning something about music. It's rather nice to learn values that are proven. It's terrible to exist only on what happens to be in the top twenty this week or whatever is the fabulous new group with the fabulous new image."

"The old men of rock, the Zeppelins and the Tulls and The Whos and the Stones, are all going on for thirty and some of them are more than thirty. And yet we're still playing, we're still selling records. It's weird as hell... There's Elton John and the Stones, who are biggest, then Zeppelin and us. One year we're bigger than them, and the next they're bigger than us. They weren't so hot a couple of years back but they are now. The Who, when they choose to tour or record, are right up there as well. But they're peculiar because of *Tommy*. It's strange but a lot of people don't know who The Who are, apart from *Tommy*."

"But there are lots of groups this year who are as big as we were five years ago who may continue to grow against all odds. Because it is against all odds. Can you imagine how difficult it is to be one of the Rolling Stones? They've been going for over ten years. Can you imagine how difficult it is to be Mick Jagger or Keith Richards and thinking, 'Christ, what are we going to do for the next album?' They can't do anything too radically different than they've done before. They've got to stay within the Stones' style and it's very, very hard to write songs that are as succinct, as oozing with immediacy, as the songs they wrote six or seven years ago. Obviously, it's a terrible struggle."

Anderson told *Cash Box* in December 1978; "I think that only by constantly testing the system you are in, by prodding it from the inside even if you make yourself unpopular by doing that, that a revitalisation takes place allowing new talent and ideas to come in. I'm not calling for urban guerrillas, but in the back of the artist's mind he should be aware of his responsibility to nudge the walls a little bit, to keep everybody on their toes... I want to continue to make music. Sometimes the process is fun, sometimes it's painful, but as a kind of work it is intuitively exciting, soft of creative on a lofty plane. I don't feel I've done it yet as well as I can and I feel I have a lot left to give, so I'm going to keep doing it."

The 2015 40th Anniversary Edition of *Minstrel In The Gallery* is well worth a listen. As with other special edition albums that Steven Wilson has worked on, there is lots of fascinating bonus stuff, including a booklet with lyrics and interviews. Two CDs and two DVDs are included. They contain the original album and seven bonus tracks, six of which were previously unreleased.

There is also nearly nine minutes' worth of footage of Jethro Tull performing 'Minstrel In The Gallery' at the Olympia in Paris in July 1975. This is a pretty big deal considering that in several interviews, band members have stated that the song is difficult to do justice to as a live piece. Equally interesting, this is a live performance of the song prior to the release of the album.

During the show, the band also play many classics from previous albums including 'War Child', 'Thick As A Brick', 'My God' and 'Aqualung'. Even without the bonus material, of which there is plenty, the 40th Anniversary Edition is a worthwhile purchase because it has been mixed in such a way that every instrument is presented so clearly; there is scope to hear all the different layers of each song with enhanced clarity compared to the original release (not that there's anything wrong with the original 1975 release, but, you know…).

With cynicism and/or candour, Anderson spoke of the anniversary editions in *Louder* in January 2016; "The truth is the copyright is running out on these titles, and record companies realise they can increase their dwindling profit margins by making use of these assets. They're not doing it out of the goodness of their hearts. But the winner is the public. And it's great news for the ancient artist's ego. I get to fool around from a discreet distance. But Steven Wilson's remixes are very educated and wise and thoughtful. He's a sensitive person who grew up with the Jethro Tull catalogue."

True to the message that Anderson has often advocated in favour of, he adds in the liner notes that what the listener gets from the album may be very different to what he intended when he wrote the songs and that such a thing is absolutely okay and indeed, inevitable: "As a lyric writer I think that leaving some space is an important ingredient, that you don't answer all the questions in the lyrics, you do leave the listeners to put something of themselves into the scenario and think about it in the light of their own experiences, or indeed experiences they've not yet had."

With regards to potential meanings of his lyrics, Anderson said in 1975; "I don't expect anything. They can do what they like with the lyrics. If they mean something to me, then I'm not such a complicated person that it will be totally obscure to other people. A lot of people take the lyrics only at face value but the majority of people derive some degree of meaning from the songs I write. I know that my songs have better lyrics than some of the garbage that comes out and a lot of what comes out is garbage. Most of the top forty stuff is garbage. I've just set myself a private little project writing some pop songs, trying to think of some very simple words for a song that would be a hit. It wouldn't be complicated but it would still be better than a lot of crap."

Ultimately, Anderson himself has often advocated strongly against over analysing his music. He was quoted in *Down Beat* in March 1976; "As soon as I begin to analyse my approach to playing music on stage, it then becomes a very deliberate and conscious dissemination of what I'm doing. And as soon as it becomes that, it immediately goes against the grain of the music I write and play. I don't sit down and say today I'm going to write a song that's going to be about this or that and then calculate a means of arriving at that end. Whatever I write — a forty second piece or a forty minute one — has always begun its life as a pure emotional feeling or observation. The act of building that into a finished recording is, of course, to a large extent, contrived, in as much as it's a conscious effort to derive a relationship between life and music and lyrics and put it into a sort of professionally embodied package and then sell it to the consumer and make money. All of that is a very conscious thing. I'm aware of all that, but I don't want to start getting any of that mixed up with the essence of what music is all about and the essence of what being a performer of music is all about".

In the same feature, Anderson spoke of his musical influences. It comes across that he was advocating for again, not getting too into the study of the music and to just go with the feel of it; "I'm interested in music in general and I've listened to all sorts of music a little bit, but I've never been moved by anything on a continuing basis, other than a very limited selection of some Negro blues, which I find now is still as moving to me as it ever was. And I find that some of the indigenous folk forms of England and Scotland also continue to move me. But I think perhaps because of the comparisons that have been made between what I write and the folky, traditional stuff, that I tend not to listen to any of that music at all. I certainly don't want to be a student of that kind of music; so if there's a similarity, it must remain really coincidental. It's something that I have only a passing awareness of. Since I was brought up in Edinburgh, Scotland, and I heard the bagpipes from an early age, it's a sound that rings in my ears. It becomes almost a folk memory of certain sounds and relationships of notes — a motive stirring of the blood."

In 2019 Anderson said of *Minstrel In The Gallery*; "In terms of the Jethro Tull canon, *Aqualung* has to sit right at the top of the tree. Not only regarding the quality of songs but as being 'iconic' to an audience the world over. Well, particularly back in the seventies. Then if you were to divide all the work including my solo stuff into three blocks of a) great, b) okay and c) perhaps not, then *Minstrel In The Gallery* would be in the second group and probably near the top of it. But, you know, it might be somebody else's favourite. For some that's even (the much-criticised) *A Passion Play*. Luckily everyone has different opinions, and that's what makes us all more interesting than otherwise we might be."

Indeed, taste and preference is so subjective. In September 1975, *Cash Box* asserted that *Minstrel In The Gallery* "offers some of Tull's best post *Aqualung* stuff. Check out the title cut and 'Baker Street Muse'."

Cash Box reviewed *Minstrel In The Gallery* in September 1975; "Like all Tull material, *Minstrel In The Gallery* is a combination of music and thought. But what makes this Tull outing the sculpted musical work it is, is the fact that the music has the obvious upper hand. Ian Anderson's lyrical range shows more in the way of the extrovert while the inner moments benefit from bodily underpinnings. Musically the Tull backing unit is given room to stretch out and they make the most of it. *Minstrel In The Gallery* is the type of album that will hang from a mantle piece when it's not being played."

The album was reviewed in *Billboard* in September 1975;

"One of the rare groups that holds its enthusiastic mass audience year after year turns in a new solid effort in its distinctive and familiar style. A highly energetic effort by writer/producer/ leader Ian Anderson and company, more streamlined and less grandiose in concept than recent Tull releases. No shortage of hit single possibilities on the set and that Tull sound is displayed without undue clutter. Not that the lyrics are any more basic than before, it's just that Ian Anderson's twisty melodies and flute-guitar riffs are presented more directly."

In the review, the best tracks were listed as being 'Minstrel In The Gallery', 'Black Satin Dancer', 'Baker Street Muse' and 'Requiem'.

The *Aberdeen Evening Express* review stated; "Jethro Tull will be back in the album charts in double quick time with this new LP — their best since *Aqualung*. It is dominated by Ian Anderson, but the group members are also in great fettle, emphasising that Tull are still one of the best rock bands around. Excellent."

The *Reading Evening Post* commented; "There's only one way to listen to Jethro Tull and that's with total commitment. Ian Anderson's lyrics are as deep as the music is complex. It's not an exaggeration to say that each individual listener has his own individual interpretation. This album is a more mellow creation than Tull's previous barnstorming offerings, with more use of acoustic guitar. In fact it's almost beautiful in parts, an adjective one cannot often use in describing Jethro Tull's music. But Anderson isn't mellowing by any means. He's changing, sure, but he still wields a mean pen. His suite 'Baker Street Muse', all about the seamy side of London, paints accurate pictures of the capital as it picks up all the threads from the rest of the album and weaves them up into a bitter tirade. It's a piece in typical Anderson style and is guaranteed to create yet another gold album for the band."

An excellent review that touches on the beauty of the album. It's such a subjective perspective but in the grand scheme of things, *Minstrel In The Gallery* covers such an array of melodic ideas and yet, so many of them are quickly memorable. This is the case even with, in typical Tull style, the use of many complex and shifting time signatures.

Whilst *Minstrel In The Gallery* was inspired, to some extent, by the frustrations that Ian Anderson had around the time that he made the album, the mellow moments on it certainly don't seem to negate some of the bitter lyrics in 'Baker Street Muse'. Put it this way: can a full range of emotion including anger, frustration and nonchalance be communicated with an acoustic guitar? Absolutely!

It was considered in *Ultimate Classic Rock* in June 2016; "For all intents and purposes, *Minstrel In The Gallery* was Jethro Tull's last stand where unapologetic intricate, high-concept prog-rock was concerned. The title track brought metal to the Middle Ages, as the monarch watched on with amusement. 'Cold Wind To Valhalla' blew it back across the sea, raping and pillaging like Viking warships, and 'Black Satin Dancer' was as dainty as it was bombastic. But it was on the engaging, seventeen-minute 'Baker Street Muse' suite that Ian Anderson paid a fond adieu to epic songcraft. And did he make it count."

Minstrel In The Gallery is an important part of Jethro Tull's legacy. It was the last album made with the line-up of Ian Anderson, Martin Barre, Barriemore Barlow, John Evans and Jeffrey Hammond. Whilst it would perhaps be an overstatement to call it a comeback album (Jethro Tull released an album every year prior to that), it was certainly a strong response to how the band had been slated by the media after *Passion Play*.

Minstrel In The Gallery was the product of a turbulent time for Ian Anderson and the band as a whole and it came out at a time when the very genre of prog rock was no longer on the firmest of footings. *Minstrel In The Gallery* is therefore important from a historical and commercial perspective, as well of course, in terms of what it achieved musically.

Appendices

Personnel

Jethro Tull
Ian Anderson — vocals, flute, acoustic guitar
Martin Barre — electric guitar
John Evan — piano, organ
Jeffrey Hammond — bass guitar, string bass
Barriemore Barlow — drums, percussion

Additional Personnel
David Palmer — string quintet arrangements and conducting
Rita Eddowes, Elizabeth Edwards, Patrick Halling and Bridget Procter — violin
Katharine Tullborn — cello

Brian Ward — photographs
Ron Kriss and Joe Garnett — front cover, based on a print by Joseph Nash
Robin Black — sound engineering

Time Signatures

Minstrel In The Gallery strikes a good balance in terms of song lengths. Whilst it's certainly not structurally what *Thick As A Brick* was (not that it was trying to be), there is that classic Jethro Tull creative use of time signatures going on. By referring to the *Minstrel In The Gallery* songbook published by Chrysalis in 1976, I've made lists of the time signatures used in each song and where they occur (so basically the lyrics that they correspond with). I'm sorry to say that it is an extremely rare songbook, definitely a collector's item (I wish a reprint was available!) but for now at least, the time signature information is definitely worthy of sharing here in this book.

Minstrel In The Gallery
The song is basically in common time with the exception of very occasional use of 2/4.

4/4 "The minstrel in the..."
2/4 "panel" 4/4 "beaters..."
2/4 "friends he'd" 4/4 "made..."

Requiem
4/4 throughout

Black Satin Dancer
6/8 "Come let me..."

3/8 "man-do" 6/8 "lin..."
(the note corresponding with "lin" holds for one bar of 6/8 and one bar of 5/8 before the song returns to 6/8 again).

There's an instrumental section that covers the following time signatures; 4/4, 5/4 for one bar, 7/8 for one bar. Then "Black satin dancer" comes in at 4/4 (the phrase "black satin dancer" spans 4/4, 5/4 then 7/8 across three separate bars.

Back to 4/4 for "tearing life from..."
7/8 "looking sweeter"
4/4 "than the brightest"
5/4 "flower"
7/8 "my garden"
Instrumental in 3/4
6/8 "come let me..."

Cold Wind To Valhalla
Cut common time (the symbol is a carry-over from the notational practice of late-Medieval and Renaissance music).
After "angels of the night" there's a 5/4 bar before cut common time resumes.
5/4 "bite" — one bar then cut common time resumes again.
5/4 "flight" — one bar then cut common time resumes once more.

One White Duck/010= Nothing At All
3/4 until one 4/4 bar for "one white duck on your wall"
Then 3/4 again
There are single 2/4 bars for the following syllables; "ter all", "at all", "sat-ion" and "fus-ion"

Baker Street Muse
4 until "symphony..." which is in 3/4. The same applies for other verses (so "symphony..." and "fertile...")

All of the following have a single 2/4 bar straight afterwards before 4/4 resumes; "breath out of time", "be your head line" and "your burial mound"

There's a single 2/4 bar prior to the start of the 'Pig-Me And The Whore' section which is in 4/4

'Nice Little Tune' is in 4/4

'Crash-Barrier Waltzer' is in 3/4

'Mother England Reverie' starts in 4/4
2/4 "wishing" 4/4 "bones"
2/4 "motor car" for one bar then back to 4/4
2/4 "public" 4/4 "bar"
2/4 "one band" 4/4 "man"
2/4 "hundred" 4/4 "grand"

The melisma on "brain" continues into a single 2/4 bar then 4/4 resumes. The same applies with the melisma on "names". The same happens with the melisma on "hands" but it's a 3/4 bar rather than a 2/4 bar.

There's a single 2/4 bar between "out of time" and "you can call me"

Grace
3/4 throughout

Track Listing

All tracks written by Ian Anderson, except track one which was written by Ian Anderson and Martin Barre. Arrangements for string quintet were written by David Palmer.

Side One
1. Minstrel In The Gallery (8:13)
2. Cold Wind To Valhalla (4:19)
3. Black Satin Dancer (6:52)
4. Requiem (3:45)

Side Two
1. One White Duck/010= Nothing At All (4:37)
2. Baker Street Muse (16:39)
3. Grace (0:37)

Total length: 45:11

*****

2002 Remaster Additional Tracks

8. Summerday Sands (3:45)
9. March The Mad Scientist (1:49)
10. Pan Dance (3:26)
11. Minstrel In The Gallery (Live) (2:12)
12. Cold Wind To Valhalla (Live) (1:31)

*****

2015 40th Anniversary Edition Tracks

CD 1: Steven Wilson stereo remix of the album and associated recordings

1. Minstrel in the Gallery (8:17)
2. Cold Wind To Valhalla (4:18)
3. Black Satin Dancer (6:54)
4. Requiem (3:43)
5. One White Duck/010= Nothing At All (4:40)

6. Baker Street Muse: Baker Street Muse (5:09)
7. Baker Street Muse: Pig-Me And The Whore (1:30)
8. Baker Street Muse: Nice Little Tune (1:09)
9. Baker Street Muse: Crash-Barrier Waltzer (3:09)
10. Baker Street Muse: Mother England Reverie (5:46)
11. Grace (0:37)
12. Summerday Sands (3:42)
13. Requiem (Early Version) (3:43)
14. One White Duck (Take 5) (2:26)
15. Grace (Take 2) (0:41)
16. Minstrel In The Gallery (BBC Version) (8:27)
17. Cold Wind To Valhalla (BBC Version) (4:22)
18. Aqualung (BBC Version) (8:01)

CD 2: Jakko Jakszyk stereo remix of the Live at The Palais des Sports, Paris, 5 July 1975 concert

1. Introduction (The Beach Part II) (0:54)
2. Wind Up (3:02)
3. Critique Oblique (4:05)
4. Wondr'ing Aloud (5:16)
5. My God including God Rest Ye Merry Gentlemen / Bourée / Quartet / Living In The Past / Thick As A Brick / My God (reprise) (11:35)
6. Cross-Eyed Mary (4:05)
7. Minstrel In The Gallery (9:24)
8. Skating On The Thin Ice Of The New Day (4:39)
9. Bungle In The Jungle (3:17)
10. Aqualung (9:41)
11. Guitar Improvisation (3:29)
12. Back-Door Angels (6:07)
13. Locomotive Breath with improvisation and including Hard-Headed English General / Back-Door Angels (reprise) (11:51)

Discography

UK
Original 5th September releases:
Chrysalis CHR 1082, LP
Chrysalis ZCHR 1082, cassette

Reissues:
Chrysalis CCD 1082, CD, 1983
Chrysalis 202 662, LP, 1987
Chrysalis CDP 32 1082 2, CD, 1992
Chrysalis 7243 5 41572 2 6, CD, 2002
Chrysalis 0825646157204, 4-disc box set, 2015
Chrysalis 0825646157198, LP, 2015

USA
Original releases:
Chrysalis CHR 1082, LP
Chrysalis – CH4 1082, LP*
*Promo, Test Pressing, Quadraphonic, never commercially released.
Chrysalis CHR M5C 1082, cassette
Chrysalis PVT 41082, cassette (club edition)
Chrysalis Y8HR 1082, 8-track
Chrysalis M8C 1082, 8-track

Reissues:
Chrysalis VK 41082, CD, 1986
Chrysalis F2 21082, CD, 1992
Chrysalis 72435-41572-2-6, CD, 2002
Chrysalis RP2 157181, CD, 2015

SINGLE

Minstrel In The Gallery / Summerday Sands
Chrysalis CHS 2075, 22nd August 1975, UK
Chrysalis CRS 2106, August 1975, USA

Tour Dates

1974

Thursday 25th July	The Centennial Hall, Adelaide, Australia
Sunday 28th July	The Festival Hall, Melbourne, Australia
Monday 29th July	The Festival Hall, Melbourne, Australia
Tuesday 30th July	The Sydney Opera House, Sydney, Australia
Wednesday 31st July	The Sydney Opera House, Sydney, Australia
Thursday 1st August	The Festival Hall, Brisbane, Australia
Friday 2nd August	The Festival Hall, Brisbane, Australia
Saturday 3rd August	The Hordern Pavilion, Sydney, Australia
Sunday 4th August	The Hordern Pavilion, Sydney, Australia
Monday 5th August	The Hordern Pavilion, Sydney, Australia
Saturday 10th August	The Civic Theatre, Auckland, New Zealand
Sunday 11th August	The Civic Theatre, Auckland, New Zealand
Monday 12th August	The Town Stage Hall, Christchurch, New Zealand
Tuesday 13th August	The Town Stage Hall, Christchurch, New Zealand
Saturday 17th August	The Kosei Nenkin Kaikan, Tokyo, Japan
Sunday 18th August	The Nagoya City Koukaido, Nagoya, Japan
Monday 19th August	The Nagoya City Koukaido, Kyoto, Japan
Wednesday 21st August	The Kaikan Dai Hall, Osaka, Japan
Friday 23rd August	The NHK Hall, Tokyo, Japan
Saturday 24th August	The NHK Hall, Tokyo, Japan
Sunday 25th August	The NHK Hall, Tokyo, Japan
Monday 26th August	The NHK Hall, Tokyo, Japan
Wednesday 28th August	The NHK Hall, Tokyo, Japan
Saturday 12th October	The Ahoy Hall, Rotterdam, Holland
Sunday 13th October	The Voorst National, Brussels, Belgium
Monday 14th October	The Voorst National, Brussels, Belgium
Wednesday 16th October	The Palais Des Sportes, Grenoble, France
Thursday 17th October	The Palais Des Sportes, Grenoble, France
Friday 18th October	Marseille, France *(unconfirmed)*
Saturday 19th October	The Parc Des Expositions, Colmar, France
Wednesday 23rd October	The Pabellon De Desportes, Madrid, Spain
Thursday 24th October	The Pabellon De Desportes, Madrid, Spain
Friday 25th October	The Pabellon De Desportes, Madrid, Spain
Saturday 9th November	The Usher Hall, Edinburgh, Scotland
Sunday 10th November	The Usher Hall, Edinburgh, Scotland
Monday 11th November	The Apollo Theatre, Glasgow, Scotland
Tuesday 12th November	The Apollo Theatre, Glasgow, Scotland
Wednesday 13th November	The Odeon, Newcastle, England
Thursday 14th November	The Rainbow Theatre, London, England
Friday 15th November	The Rainbow Theatre, London, England
Saturday 16th November	The Rainbow Theatre, London, England
Sunday 17th November	The Rainbow Theatre, London, England
Monday 18th November	The Colston Hall, Bristol, England
Tuesday 19th November	The Odeon, Birmingham, England
Wednesday 20th November	The Odeon, Birmingham, England
Thursday 21st November	The Empire Theatre, Liverpool, England
Friday 22nd November	The Opera House, Manchester, England
Saturday 23rd November	The Opera House, Manchester, England
Sunday 24th November	The New Theatre, Oxford, England
Monday 25th November	The Capitol Theatre, Cardiff, Wales
Tuesday 26th November	The Guildhall, Portsmouth, England *(cancelled)*

Tuesday 26th November	The Gaumont Theatre, Southampton, England
Saturday 30th November	The Scandinavium, Gothenburg, Sweden
Sunday 1st December	Malmo, Sweden *(unconfirmed)*
Monday 2nd December	The Olympen, Lund, Sweden
Wednesday 4th December	The Falkonerteatret, Copenhagen, Denmark
Thursday 5th December	The Falkonerteatret, Copenhagen, Denmark

1975

Friday 17th January	The Asheville Civic Centre, Asheville, USA
Sunday 19th January	The Memorial Coliseum, Tuscaloosa, USA
Monday 20th January	The Atlanta Omni, Atlanta, USA
Tuesday 21st January	The Mid South Coliseum, Memphis, USA
Wednesday 22nd January	The City State Fairgrounds, Oklahoma City, USA
Thursday 23rd January	The Convention Centre Arena, Fort Worth, USA
Friday 24th January	Hemisfair Convention Centre Arena, San Antonio, USA
Sunday 26th January	The Assembly Centre, Tulsa, USA
Monday 27th January	The Pershing Auditorium, Lincoln, USA
Tuesday 28th January	The Kemper Arena, Kansas City, USA
Wednesday 29th January	The Arena, St Louis, USA
Friday 31st January	The San Diego Sports Arena, San Diego, USA
Saturday 1st February	The San Diego Sports Arena, San Diego, USA
Sunday 2nd February	The Selland Arena, Fresno, USA
Monday 3rd February	The LA Forum, Inglewood, USA
Tuesday 4th February	The LA Forum, Inglewood, USA
Wednesday 5th February	The Community Centre Arena, Tuscon, USA
Thursday 6th February	El Paso Civic Centre, El Paso, USA
Saturday 8th February	The LA Forum, Inglewood, USA
Sunday 9th February	The LA Forum, Inglewood, USA
Monday 10th February	The LA Forum, Inglewood, USA
Sunday 16th February	Dane County Coliseum, Madison, USA
Monday 17th February	The Metropolitan Sports Centre, Minneapolis, USA
Tuesday 18th February	The Assembly Hall Illinois University, Champaign, USA
Wednesday 19th February	The Chicago Stadium, Chicago, USA
Thursday 20th February	The Chicago Stadium, Chicago, USA
Friday 21st February	The Richfield Coliseum, Cleveland, USA
Sunday 23rd February	The International Convention Centre, Niagara Falls USA
Monday 24th February	The War Memorial Centre, Syracuse, USA
Tuesday 25th February	The Spectrum, Philadelphia, USA
Wednesday 26th	The Spectrum, Philadelphia, USA
Thursday 27th February	The Hershey Park Arena, Hershey, USA
Friday 28th February	The Hampton Roads Coliseum, Hampton Roads, USA
Sunday 2nd March	The Veterans Memorial Coliseum, New Haven, USA
Monday 3rd March	The Nassau Coliseum, Uniondale, USA
Tuesday 4th March	The Nassau Coliseum, Uniondale, USA
Wednesday 5th March	The Civic Arena, Pittsburgh, USA
Thursday 6th March	The Spectrum, Philadelphia, USA
Friday 7th March	The Madison Square Garden, New York, USA
Saturday 8th March	The Providence Civic Centre, Providence, USA
Sunday 9th March	The Baltimore Civic Centre, Baltimore, USA
Monday 10th March	The Madison Square Garden, New York, USA
Tuesday 11th March	The Springfield Civic Centre, Springfield, USA
Wednesday 12th March	The Boston Tea Gardens, Boston, USA
Thursday 13th March	The Boston Tea Gardens, Boston, USA
Sunday 30th March	The Deutschlandhalle, Berlin, Germany
Tuesday 1st April	The Ostseehalle, Kiel, Germany

Saturday 5th April	The Festhalle, Frankfurt, Germany
Monday 7th April	The Sporthalle, Cologne, Germany
Tuesday 8th April	The Grugahalle, Essen, Germany
Wednesday 9th April	The Schwarzwaldhalle, Karlsruhe, Germany
Thursday 10th April	The Freidrich-Ebert-Halle, Ludwigshafen, Germany
Friday 11th April	The Festhalle, Frankfurt, Germany
Monday 14th April	The Hala Pionir, Beograd, Yugoslavia
Tuesday 15th April	The Hala Tivoli, Ljubljana, Yugoslavia
Wednesday 16th April	The Dom Sportova, Zagreb, Yugoslavia
~~Thursday 17th April~~	~~The Wienstadthalle, Vienna, Austria~~
Friday 18th April	The Olympiahalle, Munich, Germany
Sunday 20th April	The Hallenstadion, Zurich, Switzerland
Sunday 29th June	The Congress Centrum Hall, Hamburg, Germany
Monday 30th June	The Munsterlandhalle, Munster, Germany
Tuesday 1st July	The Munsterlandhalle, Munster, Germany
Wednesday 2nd July	The Phillipshalle, Düsseldorf, Germany
Thursday 3rd July	Sportshalle, Boblingen, Germany
Saturday 5th July	The Palais Des Sportes, Paris, France
Thursday 24th July	Pacific National Exhibition Coliseum, Vancouver, Canada
Saturday 26th July	The Memorial Coliseum, Portland, USA
Sunday 27th July	The Seattle Coliseum, Seattle, USA
Monday 28th July	The Oakland Coliseum, Oakland, USA
Wednesday 30th July	The Salt Palace, Salt Lake City, USA
Friday 1st August	The Dallas Convention Centre, Dallas, USA
Saturday 2nd August	The Sam Houston Coliseum, Houston, USA
Sunday 3rd August	The Madison Square Garden, New York, USA
Wednesday 6th August	The Nashville Municipal Auditorium, Nashville, USA
Thursday 7th August	The Boutwell Auditorium, Birmingham, USA
Saturday 9th August	The Coliseum, Greensboro, USA
Monday 11th August	The Gardens, Louisville, USA
Tuesday 12th August	The Civic Centre, Charleston, USA
Wednesday 13th August	The Richmond Coliseum, Richmond, USA
Thursday 14th August	The Memorial Auditorium, Chattanooga, USA
Friday 15th August	The Civic Centre Coliseum, Roanoke, USA
Saturday 16th August	The Coliseum, Charlotte, USA
Sunday 17th August	The Coliseum, Macon, USA
Monday 18th August	The Von Braun Civic Centre, Huntsville, USA
Tuesday 19th August	The Carolina Coliseum, Columbia, USA
Wednesday 20th August	The Civic Coliseum, Knoxville, USA
Thursday 21st August	The Freedom Hall Civic Centre, Johnson City, USA
Saturday 23rd August	The Mississippi Coliseum, Jackson, USA
Sunday 24th August	The Municipal Auditorium, Mobile, USA
Monday 25th August	The Coliseum, Jacksonville, USA
Wednesday 27th August	The Bayfront Centre, St Petersburg, USA
Thursday 28th August	The Jai Alai Fronton, Miami, USA
Friday 29th August	The Jai Alai Fronton, Miami, USA
Saturday 30th August	The Civic Centre Arena, Lakeland, USA
Friday 26th September	The War Memorial Auditorium, Buffalo, USA
Saturday 27th September	The War Memorial Auditorium, Buffalo, USA
Monday 29th September	The Montreal Forum, Montreal, Canada
Wednesday 1st October	The Capitol Centre, Largo, USA
Thursday 2nd October	Broome County Veterans Memorial Arena, Binghamton, USA
Saturday 4th October	The Riverfront Coliseum, Cincinnati, USA
Sunday 5th October	Cobo Hall, Detroit, USA
Monday 6th October	Cobo Hall, Detroit, USA

Tuesday 7th October	The Maple Leaf Gardens, Toronto, Canada
Wednesday 8th October	The Wings Stadium, Kalamazoo, USA
Thursday 9th October	Cobo Hall, Detroit, USA
Sunday 12th October	The Jenisen Field House, East Lansing, USA
Monday 13th October	The Des Moines Veterans Stadium, Des Moines, USA
Wednesday 15th October	The Magaw Hall, Evanston, USA
Thursday 16th October	The Evans Field House, DeKalb, USA
Friday 17th October	The Indiana State University, Terre Haute, USA
Saturday 18th October	The Kansas State University, Manhattan, USA
Sunday 19th October	Joliet High School Gym, Joliet, USA
Tuesday 21st October	Horton Field House, Illinois State University, Normal, USA
Wednesday 22nd October	The Sports Arena, Toledo, USA
Thursday 23rd October	The Lafayette College Hall, Easton, USA
Friday 24th October	The Kent State University, Kent, USA
Sunday 26th October	The University Of Iowa, Iowa City, USA
Monday 27th October	The Milwaukee Arena, Milwaukee, USA
Tuesday 28th October	The Dane County Coliseum, Madison, USA
Wednesday 29th October	Omaha, USA *(unconfirmed)*
Thursday 30th October	The Fairgrounds Coliseum, Columbus, USA
Friday 31st October	The Indiana University Assembly Hall, Bloomington, USA
Saturday 1st November	The University Of Notre Dame, South Bend, USA
Sunday 2nd November	Purdue University Hall, West Lafayette, USA
Monday 3rd November	The St John Arena, Columbus, USA

By December 1975, Jethro Tull were Ian Anderson, Martin Barre, John Evan, Barriemore Barlow and John Glascock. This line-up would continue until May 1976.

In-depth Series

The In-depth series was launched in March 2021 with four titles. Each book takes an in-depth look at an album; the history behind it; the story about its creation; the songs, as well as detailed discographies listing release variations around the world. The series will tackle albums that are considered to be classics amongst the fan bases, as well as some albums deemed to be "difficult" or controversial; shining new light on them, following reappraisal by the authors.

Titles to date:

Jethro Tull - Thick As A Brick	978-1-912782-57-4
Tears For Fears - The Hurting	978-1-912782-58-1
Kate Bush - The Kick Inside	978-1-912782-59-8
Deep Purple - Stormbringer	978-1-912782-60-4
Emerson Lake & Palmer - Pictures At An Exhibition	978-1-912782-67-3
Korn - Follow The Leader	978-1-912782-68-0
Elvis Costello - This Year's Model	978-1-912782-69-7
Kate Bush - The Dreaming	978-1-912782-70-3
Jethro Tull - Minstrel In The Gallery	978-1-912782-81-9
Deep Purple - Fireball	978-1-912782-82-6
Deep Purple - Slaves And Masters	978-1-912782-83-3

Forthcoming:
Talking Heads - Remain In Light
Jethro Tull - Heavy Horses
Rainbow - Straight Between The Eyes
The Stranglers - La Folie
Alice Cooper - Love It To Death